Not Just Another
Killing in Oakland

Not Just Another Killing in Oakland

A Civil Lawyer's View Of A Murder Trial From The Jury Box

DAVID H. FLEISIG

ISBN: **1543240917**
ISBN 13: **9781543240917**
Library of Congress Control Number: **2017902722**
CreateSpace Independent Publishing Platform
North Charleston, South Carolina

I consider trial by jury as the only anchor ever yet imagined by man, by which a government can be held to the principles of its constitution.

Thomas Jefferson

Note

This is a work of nonfiction. Everything in it is true to the best of my ability and memory and the memories of others, although any errors are mine alone. Where I have quoted someone's words, they are italicized. The quoted words were spoken during trial from the witness stand, contained in audio or videotapes presented to the jury, written in documents or said to me after trial. The quotations of Gregory Gadlin's trial testimony are from the court reporter's transcript. Quotations taken from my trial notes may not be perfectly accurate.

For Valerie and Mark Meisner

Grief fills the room up of my absent child,
Lies in his bed, walks up and down with me,
Puts on his pretty looks, repeats his words,
Remembers me of all his gracious parts,
Stuffs out his vacant garments with his form...

William Shakespeare
King John

Table of Contents

Before the Trial—Cast of Characters

THERE WERE 103 murders reported in Oakland in 2011, four times the per-capita national average. African Americans make up one quarter of Oakland's population but three quarters of its murder victims. Half the victims were under twenty five years old. While police officers, judges, prosecutors and public defenders on the front lines may be inured to the mayhem, victims' families and loved ones don't have their protective scar tissue.

Evan Meisner was one of those 103. Evan was not the youngest, oldest, first or last among that year's crop of Oakland murder victims. His was not an unusually violent, notorious or newsworthy murder. There was nothing special about it for those on the front lines—it was *just another killing in Oakland*. But there was something special about the impact it had on Evan's family and loved ones. They have carried its effects since he was killed and will continue to do so for the rest of their lives. I carry a small piece too, although my role was only as Juror Nine in the trial of Evan's killer.

This book is about the case of *The People v. Gregory Gadlin*, Alameda County Superior Court Docket No. RCD 167072. It is also about how the trajectories of two very different lives crossed on March 28, 2011 and how one abruptly ended three days later.

This is not a work of fiction. It is one juror's description of events surrounding Evan Meisner's killing and the murder trial that followed. I do not know what my eleven fellow jurors would think of what I have written here. I hope someday to find out.

Evan Meisner and Gregory Gadlin

Gregory D. Gadlin was born in 1967 in Pueblo Colorado, the third of four children. He lived in Pueblo with his parents and siblings until he was seven, when his parents divorced and his father disappeared from his life. He said about his father: *My mom didn't talk about him and I didn't ask.* He moved with his mother to Oakland in 1973; she had a stroke and he was then cared for by his maternal grandmother. He lived in the Acorn Project, a rough part of Oakland. Gadlin did not claim to have suffered abuse or neglect during his childhood. He said: *It was an adventurous and learning process. I do have some fond memories.*

Perhaps by *adventurous*, Greg Gadlin meant his criminal activities, which began in 1980 when he was twelve and arrested for petty theft. Within three years he had accumulated two more juvenile convictions for resisting arrest and burglary.

In 1982 when Gadlin was fifteen he met fourteen-year-old Stephanie Bonner, who was working the Oakland streets. It was not a romantic encounter. Gadlin stepped between Stephanie and her abusive pimp and they became a couple. She described her relationship with the man she called *Spoony* this way:

> *Young and naïve, I was in love and thought Spoony would be my hero for years to come. He was a member of a notorious gang [the] Acorn Mob, and I was his mob bitch. He took care of me materially, but eventually he started beating me...I was his trophy, and if anybody even so much as looked at me, there was a beating coming—to me. (Uncovered Me, Stephanie Bonner, Tate Publishing, 2015)*

Both were caught up in gang life and it wasn't unusual for Gadlin to have a gun.

When Gadlin was fourteen he fathered a boy named Gregory Aaron Gadlin (*Junior*) with a girl associated with the gang. Gadlin would sometimes bring this infant over for Stephanie to care for. The first of Stephanie's three children with Gadlin was born when she was fifteen. None spent much time with their father.

Gadlin was seventeen when he was committed to the California Youth Authority for carrying an unregistered, loaded gun. After his release from the CYA he briefly got back together with Stephanie and their first son, Omari Gadlin. They moved in with Gadlin's sister.

> They say you can take the man out of the prison, but you cannot take the prison out of the man; every time Spoony would do his revolving-door jail time, his sister would put me out on the street, like clockwork. (*Id.*)

A year later Stephanie was pregnant with Gadlin's second son—Lawrence Jahon Gadlin. Stephanie and her two children by Gadlin were taken in by a kind neighborhood woman. Gadlin came by from time to time to give Stephanie money and have her hold his drug stash. One day Gadlin told Stephanie he wanted to *talk*, drove her to a parking lot and beat her savagely.

> I had a fractured rib, a dislocated jaw, and some permanent damage to my right eardrum. (*Id.*)

Gadlin quickly accumulated two more convictions. These carried jail time for battery and carrying a concealed weapon. He was nineteen in 1987 when he was convicted of possession of a controlled substance for sale and sent to state prison for the first time. When he was released he and Stephanie briefly reunited, leading to the birth of Brittania Gadlin— their third child.

Evan Meisner was born in 1988 while Gadlin was serving that prison sentence. Evan had two older sisters who adored him and loving parents, Mark and Valerie Meisner. They lived in an unpretentious middle class house. His mother taught elementary school; his father helped run a Day School. That same year Gadlin was released from prison after serving his term. In 1989 he was convicted of armed robbery and sentenced to another three years in state prison.

Evan was fearless as a young toddler, jumping from the high diving board at the neighborhood pool when he was three. Gadlin was serving his state prison sentence.

After Gadlin's release he was convicted of two more felonies--carrying a firearm during commission of street gang crimes in 1992 and robbery in 1995. Each led to another stint in state prison. Meanwhile Evan grew up speed skating, riding BMX bikes and skateboarding. Evan was not wild about school, but loved the outdoors.

In July 1999 Gadlin was convicted of two more felonies--armed robbery and being a felon with a firearm. He was thirty-three years old when he was sentenced to a fifteen-year state prison term. By this time, he had fathered five children with three mothers. Since he had spent most of his adult life in prison there is no reason to believe he ever acted as a "father" to any of these children. Evan was eleven years old.

Evan went through high school while Gadlin served his latest prison term. While naturally gifted in math, Evan was not comfortable or happy in classroom settings and decided to work with his hands. Starting in about 2006 Evan worked side-by-side on construction jobs with his brother-in-law Kevin, with whom he became close. Evan loved the work and was good at it.

Gadlin was released on parole from state prison in January, 2010 after serving thirteen years. Evan, twenty-one, was working for a construction company. In May, Gadlin's son Jahon was killed in a drive-by shooting. Later that year Evan and his girlfriend Carrie Tully rented a small house at 4082 Lyon St. in Oakland. Also later that year Gadlin, needing a place to stay while on parole, married Ursula Hogan and moved into her apartment at 4100 Lyon St. Gadlin, Ursula and Stephanie Bonner had known each other for many years.

In March, 2011 Carrie and Evan decided to move out of their Lyon St. rental and were preparing to turn it back to the landlord on March 31. On Monday, March 28 Evan was moving some odds and ends out onto the sidewalk for disposal when Ursula Hogan and Gadlin came by. Evan and Gadlin talked privately on the sidewalk, then again later that day by telephone.

Evan was shot and killed in his Lyon St. rental three days later.

The Author

I am a mostly retired lawyer in my late seventies. My one toe left in the closing door of this phase of my life is my service as a Judge Pro Tem, or volunteer "judge for the day" in San Francisco. There, a couple of days a month, I hear small claims cases and mediate settlements in civil matters.

Practicing law was my second career. I graduated from the University of California Berkeley law school at 41 after dropping out of the business world, where I had progressed from bench chemist to general manager of manufacturing companies. Although there were no lawyers in my family I was always interested in the law. I travelled often during my business career and eventually developed an unusual routine. If I were in Boston and had completed what had brought me there before the end of the day I would go to a nearby courthouse, ask a bailiff what interesting cases were being tried, then sit in the back of the courtroom watching until court adjourned. Then I would talk to the attorneys about their cases. I admit to still doing this and have attended courts in London, Singapore, Johannesburg, Toronto and many U.S. cities.

I became bored with my business career and increasingly thought about dropping out and going to law school. For many years that was financially impossible. Eventually I thought: *Hmm, maybe I actually could become a lawyer.* With my wife's support I signed up for the Law School Aptitude Test at thirty seven but knew I'd be competing with smart young people fresh out of college. (I had spent nine years getting an undergraduate chemistry degree in night school.) I thought I wouldn't do well enough to apply to a decent school and that would be the end of my Law School dream.

It turned out I did well on the LSAT, so applied to nearby schools I could afford. I was not optimistic about being admitted and expected their rejections would end my Law School dream. Wrong again. I was accepted to several, most importantly the University of California's Berkeley Law School, then known as Boalt Hall. It was about three miles from our home and inexpensive. Tuition was under $2000 per year; it is now more than twenty times that.

I was then Regional Manager for a chemical products manufacturing company, responsible for factories in California, Oregon and Washington. My boss, the company's Executive Vice President, was headquartered in Minneapolis. When he next came to visit I told him over lunch about my plans to resign in a couple of months to go to law school. His response was surprising. He congratulated me and said he wanted me to continue on as a consultant while in school. He asked me to let him know what hourly rate I wanted to charge. Without thinking much about it I answered: *Let's just agree on a monthly stipend. We'll do it on a handshake basis; if at any time you want to end it, that'll be fine and I'll feel free to do the same.* I named a figure and he accepted. That arrangement lasted two years and helped me survive financially without a job. The only negative was the company often called for help when I was preparing for or in the middle of exams.

Expecting howls of derision from any lawyers who might read this, I have to say I loved law school. Of course I had a lot invested in it. I had given up a well-paying job to attend and was looked forward to an uncertain future. I did know I wanted to try cases. During law school I clerked for the California Supreme Court, law firms and a local district attorney's office. The toughest decision I faced during law school was whether to accept a job offer from the Alameda County District Attorney's office or go into civil practice. I never considered working on the criminal defense side.

At forty one I was not inclined to follow a typical new lawyer's path of working a couple of years for the District Attorney or Public Defender to gain trial experience, then moving to the civil side to earn more money. I knew as a DA I would spend the twenty years I had for this second career dealing with criminals, the pain and suffering they created and the victims they left behind. I reluctantly declined the DA's offer for a civil law practice.

Law firms recruiting litigators always promised applicants they would get trial work. I knew those promises were as meaningful as politicians' campaign pledges. Thus I routinely asked lawyers interviewing me questions something like: *When was the last time you tried a case?* or *How many cases have you tried in the last five years?* Their typical answers were *none* and *none*. I turned down all those offers.

Eventually I had an interview with Pacific Gas and Electric Company, the largest utility in California. They offered me a job in their litigation department. This is called an "in-house" position because you are employed by your client, not a law firm. I accepted the PG&E job because when I graduated from law school and passed the Bar in 1981 its law department did all of the company's litigation. I chose well, because I tried my first (very small) case ten days after being sworn in. Here is one thing I remember about it: I was hired to replace a junior lawyer I later learned was utterly incompetent. One afternoon I walked down the office corridor with the lawyer I was replacing, carrying my new trial-sized briefcase. The then Head of Litigation saw us and said: *Where are you off to?* I answered: *Fresno, to try my first case.* He harrumphed: *The blind lead-ing the blind* and turned back into his office. He was right.

After that inauspicious send-off I tried many cases in state and fed-eral courts. Since about 95% of civil cases settle, much of my career was spent working up cases, settling them when that was possible and made sense and trying them when not. After a few years I was given respon-sibility for a group of litigators, later became Chief Litigation Counsel and practiced at PG&E until my retirement. But this isn't meant to be a life story, so I will move on.

Although I did not know it at the time receiving this in the mail was my invitation to what would turn out to be a profound and moving experience.

Jury Summons

Part I

Jury Selection

Day One

I LOGGED ONTO the Alameda County Court website on August 21 hoping to find I wouldn't be needed the next day. No luck. I had to show up at 8:30. I had been called many times, but never chosen to sit on a jury. I only got onto a jury panel once, but didn't last long. It was a criminal case with an eight year old witness. A DA who looked only a few years older asked for a show of hands if anyone would not find testimony from an 8-year-old as credible as testimony from an adult. I dutifully raised my hand and explained I could not agree with that proposition without knowing something about the child. I was excused about a minute and a half later.

The Rene Davidson Courthouse, Oakland

There were over two hundred people gathered in the jury assembly room in the Rene Davidson Courthouse the next morning. We were a smorgasbord of every imaginable ethnic group. The vast majority of us sat quietly, staring intently at our electronic devices.

The clerk eventually called out ninety names. While listening for mine I admired her ability to pronounce them. They were told they were "Group A" and were to report to Department 8 on the 5th floor. Those called slowly worked their way out. My name was not among them; I felt mildly optimistic I would be released. It was about 10:00 in the morning.

Soon the clerk read out another ninety names, this time including mine. We were told we were "Group B" and should also head up to Department 8 on the 5th floor. Group B filed into and filled every seat in the courtroom. (I now understood why there had been *two* panels of ninety.) I glanced up at the Judge, who looked down at us benignly.

This must be what they mean by diversity. Judge Vernon Nakahara is a short, dignified Japanese American just under 70, with a neatly trimmed beard and gray hair.

Judge Vernon Nakahara

He told us this was a murder case and the trial would take about three weeks. I looked over at the person I correctly took to be the

defendant. He was an African American man in his late 40's, 5'11"
tall, with heavily muscled shoulders and arms. The Deputy District
Attorney was Warren Ko, a Chinese American in his 30s, neatly dressed
in a conservative suit and tie. Although I did not know or suspect it
because he was so competent, Warren had only been practicing law
for seven years. The Assistant Public Defender was George Arroyo, a
Hispanic American in his 40s, who was trim, balding and nattily attired
in a suit and tie. George had been a PD twenty years and exuded confi-
dence and competence.

Judge Nakahara told us this case involved a March, 2011 murder and
the defendant's name was Gregory Gadlin. I puzzled over why it had
taken five years for the case to get to trial. It did not occur to me this
might be a retrial. I thought about Googling *Gadlin* and then realized
I could not do so without violating the judge's admonition against con-
ducting independent research. The judge also told us the trial would
take about three weeks.

Judge Nakahara said those claiming service on the jury would be
a hardship should stay behind. He instructed the rest of us to fill out
fifteen page questionnaires and report back at 1:30.

The questionnaire included basic demographic questions about
us and our spouses, our previous jury service and any relationships we
might have with law enforcement officers. It also asked about our ownership and use of guns, whether we or close family members had been
crime victims, our hobbies and what TV programs we watched. I was
amused it asked about our news sources. I thought about writing down
what passes for politically correct in the San Francisco Bay Area—The
New York Times, The Economist, NPR, CNN, The New Yorker, MSNBC,
and Masterpiece Theatre for television, but had promised myself I would
be entirely truthful, so did not.

There was not enough time to go home and get back by 1:30, so I had a couple of hours to kill. I knew a judge in Alameda County and decided to look him up, although we had not been in contact for over twenty years. He was my divorce lawyer a long time ago and we served together later on a non-profit Board. His courtroom in a building across the street was locked and dark. While I stood there pondering what to do next, an adjacent door opened and his clerk came out. I asked if the judge were available and gave her my name. She went back inside. Surprisingly she quickly came back and escorted me in. I spent a pleasant hour renewing my acquaintanceship with the judge, then went to lunch feeling jury service was going just fine so far.

After lunch we milled about outside Department 8 for a long time while the judge dealt with people claiming jury service would be a hardship. I noticed all of the hardship claimants stayed with the rest of us after emerging from their bouts with the judge. Apparently Judge Nakahara was a hard sell for excuses from jury service. The least credible hardship claim I ever heard was made by a panel member in a case I tried in Federal Court. A woman claimed hardship because she was secretary of her bowling league, which needed her to keep track of their scores. Eventually our group was let into the courtroom. At some point a clerk read off about twenty names and told those people they had been released. We were not told why.

The judge had the ninety potential jurors left from Groups A and B aggregated together in the courtroom. I looked around and was surprised to see only three appeared to be African American. A large proportion—possibly one fourth seemed to be Asian.

The judge told us we would be off the next day—Tuesday—and must return Wednesday morning for voir dire.

Voir Dire

There were only about seventy of us left when we filed in Wednesday morning. Apparently another twenty or so potential jurors had been released on Tuesday for mysterious reasons. Now there were *no* African Americans left. Judge Nakahara explained he would fill the twelve juror seats with names selected at random. Questioning of potential jurors, or *voir dire* would then begin. (Voir Dire meant *speak the truth* in old French. Today it is the process by which the Judge and/or lawyers question potential jurors to determine whether they would be fair and impartial.) That may be the official explanation, but the reality is somewhat different. The reality reflects the players' very different goals. The judge wants a jury sufficiently representative of the community and selected in a facially neutral process to avoid higher court scrutiny. The contending lawyers want jurors they believe will vote the *right* way, i.e., for their clients.

The clerk began calling names to fill the twelve juror chairs; she called my name for seat nine. When she had filled all twelve seats Judge Nakahara began questioning the person in seat one. It quickly became clear Judge Nakahara would do most of the questioning, which surprised me. I did not like judges taking over voir dire because it was my best chance to assess potential jurors while trying to establish rapport with them. On the other hand judges have had good reason to take over. Lawyers often try to use voir dire to plant ideas in the jury panel. Imagine a DA questioning panel members in a case with a serious police search issue: *How would you feel if a guilty person got off because of a police error?*

The judge had our questionnaires in front of him and read them over before beginning questioning each panel member. I noticed both the DA and PD had arranged 3" x 5" Post-it's in front of them in a six column, two row order, matching our jury box seating positions. As the Judge began his questions, both studied their copies of our questionnaires, which I could see they had highlighted with color markers. Each occasionally jotted notes on his Post-it's as questioning continued. I could see the DA had written a few words on *my* Post-it and wondered what they were. Because in an ancient tradition the DA was seated closest to the jury I could see what he was doing, but not read what he had written. I had a poorer view of the PD across the courtroom. I saw the PD and Gadlin huddled together, looking at the questionnaires and the PD's notes. Gadlin seemed interested and involved in the process.

Judge Nakahara questioned panel members separately, spending ten to twenty minutes with each. He started with general questions to get the person talking, then focused in on any issues he had seen in the questionnaire or heard in that person's answer to one of his questions. He started with Juror One, who sat in the upper row on the left side, close to the judge and the witness box.

Potential Juror One was an Indian woman who apparently had written on her questionnaire she could not stand the sight of blood or violence. Judge Nakahara did not give up on her easily. He asked: *What do you do if something violent is shown on a TV program or movie you are watching?* She answered she avoids such situations, but if she could not, hides her face. He explained all members of the jury would have to see explicit photographs during the trial and every juror would have to look at and consider those. I could not decide whether her claimed aversion was real or a ploy to avoid jury service. It may not have been clear to Judge Nakahara either, since he told her she should think about what they had discussed and he would revisit the issues with her later.

When Judge Nakahara finished with a panel member the DA would pick up the questioning. When he finished it was the PD's turn. I listened carefully to their colloquy with Juror One, trying to figure out from their questions whether they wanted her on the jury. She disappeared the following day, so either was excused for cause (she could not look at pictures of violence or bloodshed), or the attorneys and/or judge had agreed she was not an appropriate juror for some other reason.

When both sides were finished with Juror One, Judge Nakahara moved on to Juror Two. This woman had a background managing hospitals. I guessed the PD would see her as a potential leader, not likely to be sympathetic to his client and not afraid to make decisions. I guessed he would dump her. He did.

Seat Five was occupied by a woman with many years' experience working in *touchy feely* social service jobs. I guessed the DA would see her as a soft touch, potentially sympathetic to the defendant and would dump her. He did.

A young Asian man who was an Engineer in a tech firm was in the fourth seat. He was concerned about serving in a three-week trial because he had just begun a new job and said he would only be paid for five days of jury service. After further questioning he said he could serve. But late the next day, after the final twelve jurors had been seated, he raised his hand and tried to re-open the issue. Judge Nakahara was not amused. He swatted down number Four's plea, saying he had had his chance earlier and said then he could handle the income loss.

A thirty-something Asian man in seat Seven told Judge Nakahara he did not speak English well enough to serve. This obviously annoyed the Judge, who sarcastically wondered how seat Seven had just completed an Engineering degree at Berkeley without becoming fluent enough in English to serve as a juror. Nevertheless, he was dismissed from the panel and departed.

Judge Nakahara moved on to juror Eight, an Indian-American man also in the tech industry. We later learned he had been sworn in as a U.S. citizen only ten days before arriving for jury service. Welcome new citizen! He remained on the jury and ended up leading groups of us to good ethnic restaurants on lunch breaks.

Judge Nakahara finally turned to me. I wanted to serve so I could see what it was like to be a juror, especially in a serious criminal case, but never thought I would end up on the jury.

I was determined to be completely frank and honest—to let the chips fall where they might. Judge Nakahara asked many questions about my legal work, one of which led to this amusing exchange: Judge Nakahara: *I see we both went to Berkeley Law, but you weren't sworn in until many years after I was.* (Judge Nakahara was about 70; I was 77.) I answered: *Yes, and your question is?* Everyone chuckled. He looked at me for a long moment over the top of his glasses then changed the subject. He later asked what kind of legal work I did. I answered: *I was a civil litigator.* He said: *Well, there are lots of "litigators".* I took this to imply *litigators* pushed paper around and did not know their way around the inside of a courtroom. Feeling insulted, I responded: *I tried cases in state and federal courts across California.* He seemed surprised and opened a new front: *There are lots of differences between state and federal courts. Yes, there are* I answered, while silently pondering whether to add my opinion that federal judges were generally better prepared and more competent than their state counterparts. Prudence prevailed; I stayed silent.

The DA did not have many questions for me. One was: *You've seen lawyers you thought were good, and some you thought not so good....* I interrupted and interjected: *Judges too.* This got my second voir dire chuckle. I did not look up to see Judge Nakahara's response. I wondered if the DA's brief questioning suggested he wanted me on the jury and didn't want to risk what I might say. Later a private criminal defense attorney friend guessed it was more likely I would be dumped by the DA than the PD. He said DAs generally wanted jurors to rely on *them*, rather than a lawyer-juror who might be a leader during deliberations.

After we had rendered our verdict three weeks later a juror asked the DA why he had left a lawyer (me) on the panel. The DA answered: *He was a civil lawyer for PG&E, so it wasn't a factor.* Although Warren didn't mean it that way, I felt put down. I had left lawyers on juries after voir dire when I felt they would be fair. Trial lawyers are always more cautious about potential jurors they assess as potential leaders during deliberations.

DA Ko told me something funny and intuitively true after trial. He was not concerned about having *one* lawyer on the jury but would never leave *two* on, because two lawyers wouldn't agree about anything.

The PD asked me the toughest question I got during voir dire. How would I handle a situation during deliberations if other jurors said: *You're a lawyer, what does this instruction mean?* I wasn't expecting this and answered as truthfully as I could, saying I would be there to follow the Court's instructions. If the jury had to figure out what an instruction meant, I certainly would do that for myself. If asked, I would tell other jurors how I understood the instruction as a juror, not lawyer. As these words came out of my mouth I realized what a fine line I was drawing. The PD seemed satisfied with my answer. Questioning then moved on to the final three jurors.

Eventually there were twelve of us in the box who had been questioned by the judge and both attorneys. The attorneys started with *peremptory* challenges, meaning they needed no excuse to get rid of someone. I realized Judge Nakahara had not explained that process to us. Both the DA and PD used the standard verbiage: *The [people] [defense] thank and excuse Juror One.*

After each challenge the clerk called a new name from the approximately twenty panel members left in the back of the room. I remembered my experiences picking juries. I would look back at who was left in the panel then quickly have to decide whether to use up one of my remaining challenges to swap a juror in the box for an unknown from the back of the room. Judge Nakahara began questioning each newly seated potential juror and was then followed by counsel. When that was completed the opportunity to exercise a peremptory moved to whichever attorney's turn it was: *The defense thanks and excuses Juror Two.*

My pulse rate increased every time the DA or PD rose to exercise a challenge. Every time I expected to hear: *The [people/defense] thank and excuse Juror Nine.* There had been about fifteen peremptory challenges and I hadn't heard those words yet.

Eventually the DA said: *Pass the jury,* meaning he had chosen not to exercise another peremptory challenge. I knew if the PD did the same the peremptory challenge process would be over and we twelve remaining would become the jury. I also knew one side could pass, then after a peremptory by the other side, reenter the fray and use another challenge. During a break one panel member asked me if he could still be challenged although questioning and challenging had moved beyond him. I thought about whether it was appropriate for me to answer a question like that, then told him: *Yes,* and explained the theory is seating a new juror could affect the lawyers' assessments of the panel's overall balance.

After trial I learned each side had been given twenty peremptory challenges to use for the twelve jurors to be selected. The DA and PD each used about nine, so neither fired all their arrows. I was surprised to hear both sides had been given the order in which panel members would be called to fill empty slots. For example, they knew Mr. Smith was next in line to be seated, Ms. Jones after that, etc. My experience in both federal and state courtrooms was quite different, with the court clerk randomly picking a name each time a slot became available. Judge Nakahara's method made it much easier for the lawyers to execute their jury selection strategy. Counsel had read and highlighted the panels' questionnaires before we got to this point. As voir dire continued they only had to review those of the next few names to be called when deciding whether to challenge a seated juror. That process is roughly analogous to deciding whether to stick with the devil you know.

We twelve who survived voir dire were made up of two Hispanics, four Asians (Chinese and Indian) and six who would be categorized as white by those who count that way. Sliced differently, there were six jurors working in computer or technical jobs, one chemist, one biologist, one children's special needs counselor, one bank employee, one office worker and one retired lawyer---me.

There were no African Americans on the jury in this heavily African American county. After trial the PD told me Gadlin had commented about there being no African Americans on his first jury. The Alameda County Public Defenders' office had raised the issue in the past. But after a thorough review of county policies and statistics reluctantly accepted data showing that while African Americans were called for jury service in proportion to their numbers in the area most did not show up.

Late that afternoon both the DA and PD said they *passed the panel* and I realized I was actually going to serve on this jury. I began to feel the heavy weight of responsibility of sitting in judgment in a murder trial. I had not anticipated this. Judge Nakahara adjourned proceedings for the day and told us we would select the three alternates the next morning.

Judge Nakahara's practice for filling a seat if a juror became ill or was otherwise unable to continue was to elevate the first alternate to fill the slot. If another vacancy were to occur, Alternate Two would move up, and so on. Since this was only going to be a three-week trial, it seemed very unlikely anyone other than Alternate One might be elevated to juror status.

Later I learned Judge Nakahara had allowed each side only three peremptory challenges for alternates. Filling the first seat turned out to be an lengthy process. At least three potential jurors for the most important first alternate seat were questioned, challenged and replaced.

One was a Chinese man in his seventies who spoke very broken English. Based on Judge Nakahara's questions, he apparently had revealed many health problems in his questionnaire. I wondered how well he would understand the proceedings and if he were among the jurors how he could meaningfully participate in deliberations. Fortunately the issue became moot; Judge Nakahara dismissed him.

The next up was someone we could not avoid having noticing as we milled about the hallway before court or during recesses. He was a slender white man about fifty, with a bald head surrounded by a fringe of stringy hair hanging down to his shoulders. His eyes bounced around with no fixed focus, amplifying the impact of his facial expressions, which varied between excitement and mania. He carried his laptop everywhere, working away at it in the hallways. He told the Judge he needed to eat every hour or so. The Judge dryly told him that would not be a problem. It was clear to me he would be challenged—the only question was by whom. The DA questioned him perfunctorily. I guessed because he knew he would have to challenge him and hoped the PD would do so first. Since the PD would be happy to have had someone seated who could instigate a hung jury, he asked a few even more perfunctory questions and sat down. This forced the DA to exercise one of his three challenges: *The People thank and excuse Alternate One.*

He was replaced by a tall, slender, elegantly dressed and soft spoken man in his thirties born in the Philippines. He told Judge Nakahara his brother was in state prison and he had come to believe incarceration was not the way to deal with criminal behavior. I glanced at the DA, who maintained a poker face, but I knew this guy was toast. *The people thank and excuse Alternate One.* Although I didn't know it at the time, this was the DA's last peremptory for the three alternate slots. Using up your last peremptory challenge is a tough move for a trial lawyer. You can only pray whoever takes the now open seat is better than those you had challenged.

True confession--trial lawyers can be unkind to each other. Here is a situation where I was. I had a case where I had had many conflicts before trial with another defendant's attorney. The judge had split peremptories between us and the other defense attorney eventually used up all of his. I had not. The next panelist called up was obviously a terrible juror for a defendant (young, unclean looking, straggly long hair, baggy jeans, wearing a Grateful Dead tee shirt.) As the *Deadhead* strutted up the aisle to take his seat, the *frenemy* lawyer sitting next to me frantically whispered in my ear I had to challenge him. I innocently asked: *Why, what's wrong with him?* I then questioned the new juror for a while just to torture my disagreeable seatmate, then dumped the Deadhead.

The DA's gamble paid off. The Alternate One slot was filled with a reasonable appearing and sounding Hispanic-American man in his early thirties who worked at a local casino. The Alternate Two slot was filled with *Jimmy*, a Chinese-American man in his twenties who had recently graduated from college. Jimmy had worked as a clerk at several law firms, was studying for the LSAT and hoped to become a lawyer. He was an enthusiastic participant throughout trial. He took copious notes and often submitted written questions for Judge Nakahara to ask witnesses. Jimmy told me after trial that when the jury had been sent to deliberate he asked Judge Nakahara if he could sit with us *to observe*. The answer was a firm *no*.

The third alternate slot was finally filled with a woman in her mid-twenties with an interesting background. She had been removed from her home as a child because of parental abuse and had grown up in foster care. She had a job working with young people with similar backgrounds. Since I am an enthusiastic volunteer for "CASA" (Court Appointed Special Advocates), a non-profit which helps kids just like that, I asked her during a break if while in foster care she had had a CASA volunteer. Sadly, she had not.

It took until after lunch Thursday afternoon to get the three alternates seated. We had shown up Monday morning, so the jury selection process had taken four days.

My friend Bill is a sole practitioner criminal defense lawyer in Alameda County. During the jury selection process I had told Bill I was temporarily seated as a prospective juror in Judge Nakahara's courtroom. After trial Bill told me he called PD Arroyo and told him he knew someone on the panel. Bill told the PD something like: *This guy is smart, if you've got a defense and he buys it, he won't be moved and likely would bring others with him. On the other hand, if he thinks your defense is BS, he'll see through it and bring others with him that way.* After trial I asked the PD why he had left me on the panel. The PD related his conversation with Bill and said he wanted at least one strong juror who, while perhaps thinking his client was guilty, would feel compelled to vote *not guilty* if the DA had failed to prove the prosecution's case beyond a reasonable doubt. Thus he left me on--but was surprised the DA hadn't challenged me. George also told me after trial my voir dire exchanges with Judge Nakahara convinced him I would end up as foreman if I stayed on the panel.

Judge Nakahara told the jury to consider the courtroom *a box.* We were only to consider what we heard, read or saw inside that box. I thought that a useful metaphor and reminded jurors about it during deliberations when someone speculated about facts not presented *inside the box* during trial.

Judge Nakahara excused us until Monday morning when we would hear counsel's opening statements.

A Courtroom Just Like Judge Nakahara's
My Seat Was Third From the Easel, on the Lower Level

As sworn jurors we were told to go directly to the jury deliberation room when we arrived and after breaks. It was on the floor above our courtroom and linked to it by a private stairway behind the table seating the defendant and his PD. (The left side of the table in the photograph. The DA occupied the right side of the table, closest to the jury box.)

The PD and DA stood respectfully as the jury entered and left the courtroom. Then everyone stood when Judge Nakahara entered. This tradition added to the solemnity of the proceedings and the weight of responsibility I felt. I assumed the other jurors felt the same way, but never discussed it with them.

Part II

Trial

Opening Statements

DISTRICT ATTORNEY Ko took us through Evan Meisner's killing in detail. He used pictures, maps, physical evidence, (including the pistol he claimed would be proven to be the murder weapon), portions of a recorded phone call made by Gadlin after his arrest and telephone call records linking Gadlin with Evan. He said near the end of his statement:

> *Evan Meisner was shot in the neck and murdered over a bag of marijuana he would have handed over gladly*

It was apparent how much technology had improved in the years since I last tried a case. Photographs and other visual evidence were projected from the DA's computer onto two large HD screens easily seen by the jury. The DA took about an hour for his opening, concluding:

> *At the conclusion of this trial I will be asking you to return a verdict of guilty of murder in the first degree.*

Public Defender Arroyo told us *other versions of events* would come out during trial. He implied Evan was killed by a friend named Rodney, with whom Evan was going to do a drug deal, not Gadlin. He said Rodney had given conflicting versions of what happened over time and had told the police he saw Evan alive *after* the time the prosecution said the murder occurred. He pointed out there would be no fingerprint or DNA evidence on the gun in question. The PD then said there would be alibi witnesses testifying Gadlin was home at the time of the crime.

The PD took about forty five minutes, concluding Opening Statements. It was now noon and we broke for lunch with the DA set to begin presenting evidence when we returned.

Jury Interaction Outside the Courtroom

We had been instructed to be in court before 9:30 every morning. After having been sworn in as the jury we were led to the deliberation room by Bervin Hankins, the Sheriff's Deputy in charge of the jury. Bervin is an African American man, perhaps fifty years old. He is over six feet tall and muscular. His demeanor varied between professionally serious and smilingly paternal.

The jury deliberation room is a joyless, graceless, typical government space, probably last painted decades ago. It was about ten by twenty feet, with a conference table long enough to fit twelve chairs—four on each side and two at each end, with more arranged against the walls. There was a small refrigerator and coffee maker, both of which we put to good use. We also had our own bathrooms. One diverting feature of the room was a supposedly centrally-set wall-mounted clock. It was always off by some random number of hours. Many of us played with trying to get it set to the right time. We would set it properly when we convened in the morning but by lunch it would have drifted off onto Singapore time, or that of some other mysterious place. The room's saving grace was its large window at the far end looking out on Lake Merritt and an adjoining park. The second saving grace was that it opened.

Jurors started arriving at about 8:30. Cameron, an early arriver and newly minted chemist, took it upon himself to clean the coffee pot and make fresh coffee. Most jurors sat quietly, looking at their cellphones, tablets and laptops before we were called down to the courtroom. A few jurors used their laptops to keep up with work. The others read email or surfed the web. Of course the judge had repeatedly ordered us to not look up anything related to the case. Only I and one or two others read old fashioned (not electronic) books or newspapers. The young woman who was Alternate Three meticulously filled in intricate patterns in coloring books with an array of colored pens. We all admired her work. There wasn't much conversation.

We had breaks of about fifteen minutes in the mid-morning and mid-afternoon. That wasn't enough time to leave the courthouse so we hung out in the deliberation room. Lunch was typically an hour and a half. I went out with one to six other jurors to local Thai, Indian or coffee shop-type places in the neighborhood. The area around the courthouse could be described as run down urban, with street people hanging about and a number of boarded up shops. There were one or two new places with expensive coffee served by and mostly to heavily tattooed twenty-somethings. You would not want to walk around this neighborhood after dark.

I never became aware that any juror violated Judge Nakahara's admonitions during the three and a half weeks of trial. Before we began deliberations I saw no juror discuss anything about the case other than speculating about how long the trial was going to last, or whether they would be able to make it to a scheduled business meeting. Surprisingly I did not hear anyone complain about the burden of their jury service on their work or family obligations.

The People's Case: Gregory Gadlin Murdered Evan Meisner

Evan Meisner was twenty two years old in March, 2011. He was white and slender at 160 lbs. and just under six feet tall. He had a loving family; their home was about twenty miles south of Oakland. His father was Mark, his mother Valerie. His girlfriend of two years was Carrie Tully, a 27-year-old attractive young woman.

Evan and Carrie

Evan worked for a construction company for $20 an hour and moon-lighted doing small jobs like installing dry wall or tilework. In early March 2011 Evan did a bathroom remodel on his own time for someone who paid him in part with about a quarter pound of pot. Evan told Carrie he would sell the pot for rent money.

Evan and Carrie had been living together for about six months in a small rented house at 4082 Lyon Ave. in East Oakland.

This was a drug-infested, dangerous neighborhood, with gunshots heard many nights. Evan and Carrie shared the house with two room-mates. Since the rent was $1,400, each one's share was $350. The lease was due to expire on March 31. Evan had planted a vegetable garden in the large back yard. His parents, Valerie and Mark Meisner had visited Evan and Carrie there.

4082 Lyon
Evan and Carrie's Rental

Evan and Carrie both enjoyed smoking pot. They bought small quantities from and occasionally shared it with Rodney Fisher, an African American man who lived in the 8-unit apartment house next door. Rodney was the neighborhood supplier of *nickel and dime* ($5 and $10) bags of marijuana.

As you face 4082 Lyon from the street, 4100 Lyon is on the right. Rodney Fisher lived in that building. Gregory Gadlin, his wife, Ursula Hogan and Albert Pearson, her teenage son shared an apartment there as well.

In early March Evan decided he wanted his own place rather than share one with Carrie. She was not happy about Evan's decision, but accepted her five-year younger boyfriend had some maturing to do. They remained close though. The other two roommates also left in early March. Evan had given notice to their landlord and had arranged for her to pick up the keys under the front door mat the morning of March 31.

4100 Lyon
Ursula Hogan and Greg Gadlin's balcony was on the front left on the second level

Evan had rented a room on 7th Street in East Oakland for $600/month in mid-March from Lisa Pecoraro and Mike Sutz. It was about two miles from the Lyon St. house. Evan and Carrie began moving in mid-March. He and Carrie worked on cleaning out the Lyon St house to ready it for their March 31 departure.

Lisa and Mike were in their forties. They rented the 7th Street house and subleased rooms in it to help cover their rent. Some might describe Lisa and Mike as aging hippies. Lisa was an avid participant in the local music scene and augmented her income by making customized buttons with local music groups' logos and names. Mike, balding and paunchy, had no visible means of support and I wondered if he was on SSI disability. Mike was a daily medicinal pot user and apparently had grown and sold it from time to time.

Evan's new landlords did not have a checking account and had told Evan he had to pay his $600 rent in cash. His first full month's rent was due on April 1.

March 28, 2011

On Sunday March 28 Gadlin, Ursula and her fourteen-year-old son Albert Pearson returned to 4100 Lyon St from a visit to a park. They saw household belongings piled on the sidewalk in front of the house at 4082. Evan was going in and out, piling discarded stuff on the sidewalk for garbage pickup. There was a small refrigerator in the pile. Ursula wanted it and asked Evan if it was being thrown away. He said it was and she could have it. Gadlin and Evan spoke privately on the sidewalk while someone carried the refrigerator to Ursula and Gadlin's apartment. Ursula saw the two men talking but did not hear what was said. This was the first known contact between Evan and Gadlin. Evan made a brief call to Gadlin shortly after five pm that day.

Gregory Gadlin, 2011

March 29, 2011

Cell phone records showed three calls between Evan and Gadlin the next day. The first two were from Gadlin to Evan mid-day, the third was from Evan to Gadlin that evening.

March 30, 2011

On Wednesday the 30th Rodney Fisher asked Evan if he could park his car in Evan's driveway. Evan said *sure*, but told Rodney he was moving out the next day, so Rodney would have to move his car then. Rodney agreed and parked in Evan's driveway, leaving room behind him for Evan's pickup.

Steve Bocchini and Evan had been close friends since their teens. Steve was two years older than Evan and dark-haired, with a neatly trimmed beard. Although younger than Steve and his friends, Evan quickly fit in and became a leader of the group.

Evan Meisner and Steve Bocchini, 2010

Steve had visited Evan and Carrie often at 4082 Lyon St. On Wednesday March 30 Evan went to Steve's place in Berkeley in the late afternoon. They smoked some pot then went to dinner at an Indian restaurant on Telegraph Avenue.

Most of the friends' dinner conversation was about Evan's relationship with Carrie. Evan did not want to break up with Carrie, but wanted the opportunity to see other women. Evan was gregarious and had no difficulty making friends or meeting women. This debate about commitment versus freedom had been a common topic of conversation between the friends.

Evan told Steve he had gotten a quarter pound of pot in partial payment for a $600 side job and was going to sell it for rent money. Evan said he was going to sell the weed that night and hoped to get $800 for it. Steve was worried and asked if Evan knew the person he planned to it sell to. Evan said the buyer was a neighbor, *a big black guy who recently got out of jail and was on parole*, whom Evan said he had known a few weeks. Steve had never known Evan to sell marijuana before.

Steve asked Evan what he would do if the pot sale turned into a robbery. Evan said he would simply hand over the weed. He thought the worst outcome was he would lose the marijuana. Evan put on a brave front, but was worried about the marijuana sale going south. Carrie told me after the trial Evan asked several friends to go with him, but all refused because it was too dicey a proposition.

Steve told me Evan had always been fearless. He described how their group of teens had gone to a swimming hole in the mountains abutted by a 50-foot rock cliff. Steve and all the others had been there before and jumped feet first off the rocks into the lake. Although Evan had never been there he climbed to the top and did a swan dive. Evan had

no concerns about living in the dangerous Lyon Street neighborhood—
Steve was more worried about his friend living there than Evan was.

Evan told Steve he had shown the marijuana to Gadlin a couple of
days earlier and Gadlin had said he *could do something with it.* Evan said
something to Steve like: *If some crackhead gets crazy with me, I'll get crazy back.*

Evan dropped his friend off at Steve's apartment at about 10:30 pm--
the last time Steve saw Evan alive. Steve is still wracked with guilt about
not stopping Evan from going ahead with the pot sale, perhaps by buy-
ing the pot himself.

After trial the PD told me the issue of how much of Steve Bocchini's
testimony could be admitted at trial had been decided by Judge
Nakahara before trial began. The legal issue was that Evan's statements
to Steve were classic *hearsay*--Steve testifying about what Evan had said.
The hearsay rule against secondhand testimony is riddled with excep-
tions. I recall having to memorize about twenty three for the Bar Exam.
One exception was a statement by a witness not present [Evan] offered
to prove or explain [Evan's] *conduct,* or intent to do a certain act. The
DA argued Steve's testimony showed Evan's intent to sell marijuana to
a specifically described person (large, African American, neighbor, recently out of prison, on parole.) Judge Nakahara heard counsel's arguments on Steve's potential testimony about two weeks before trial and
ruled in the DA's favor. Thus Steve Bocchini was allowed to testify about
his dinner conversation with Evan.

Evan and Carrie had talked about meeting that evening at a club in
San Francisco. At 11:23 pm Evan texted Carrie asking if she wanted to
get together, Carrie responded with a text asking if Evan was going to
meet her at the club. In the last communication Carrie was to have with
him Evan texted back: *I wish.*

Evan returned to his new place on 7th Street after dropping Steve off. Mike Sutz reminded Evan he had to pay his $600 rent on April 1. Evan asked if he could pay with a check; Mike said *no.* Evan responded he would do what he could to get the cash that night.

After the trial I asked Carrie why Evan had a problem getting the $600 rent money he needed. She explained business had been slow where he worked, Evan was paid on an hourly basis and was not getting many hours of work. He also had payments to make on his pickup truck.

Evan had a plastic bag filled with pot witnesses variously described as the size of a *freezer bag*, or *turkey bag.* Mike used his own pot scale to help Evan divide it into one ounce baggies, which they then put back into the larger bag. Mike and Evan were drinking beer at about midnight. Mike told Evan not to go out to sell the pot. He said it was too dangerous to go out at that hour in this area and they could *figure out* the rent issue. He said: *Don't worry about having the rent on time.* (There would have been a $50 charge for a late rent payment.) Evan responded: *I'm a big boy and can take care of myself. I'm not worried about it.* After the trial I told Carrie what Evan had said. She smiled wryly and nodded—that was Evan.

Evan put his partly finished beer in Mike's refrigerator, took the plastic bag of pot and a basket of his laundry and left the house close to midnight. He told Mike he would be back in fifteen or twenty minutes.

The PD's cross-examination of Michael Sutz brought out that the DA had dropped pending marijuana cultivation charges against him after the *first trial.* Hearing that exchange was how I learned this was a retrial.

March 31, 2011
Cell phone records showed eight calls between Evan and Gadlin on March 31; four initiated by each. Gadlin made the first at 12:13 am.

Evan made the last at 1:29 am, which was unanswered. With Evan not having returned, Lisa and Mike repeatedly called Evan's cell after 1:00 am. No one answered.

Willie Carter and Rodney Fisher lived in the 4100 Lyon Street apartment house next door. They knew each other as neighbors. Both described their acquaintanceship as one of *hi and by*. Willie occasionally bought nickel or dime bags of pot from Rodney. (Hi and buy?)

At 1:40 am Willie called Rodney and said he had heard a noise like a gunshot or car tire exploding. Rodney had heard the same thing and was concerned about his car parked in Evan's driveway. The timing of and parties to that call were verified by the detective who knocked on Rodney's door the next day investigating Evan's murder. When Rodney told him about the call, the detective verified the details by examining the call log on Rodney's cell phone. After hearing the noise Rodney went outside to check on his car in Evan's driveway.

Rodney was reinteviewed by Sgt. Gantt a year after the murder—an encounter both described as an *intense*. Rodney for the first time said he had seen a man run through the back yard of Evan's house and climb over the back fence into the adjacent park. Rodney repeated that at trial. He said he could not see the person's face, but described him as a male African American Gadlin's size. Rodney had not said anything to the police the day after the murder about this backyard sighting. The jury later discounted all of Rodney's testimony.

Evan was killed by a 9mm bullet fired into the side of his neck just below his left ear, in an almost horizontal path. The gun muzzle was inches from Evan's neck when the shot was fired, leaving telltale *stippling* around the entry wound. There was no exit wound. The bullet severed Evan's cervical spinal cord and killed him virtually instantaneously. Bullet fragments were later recovered from Evan's spinal cord. There were no signs of defense wounds--no trauma or injury to Evan's hands or anywhere else on his body.

Evan's body lay face down on the floor between the bedroom and living room. He was killed there; there was no evidence his body had been moved. There were bloodstains on the bottom twelve inches of the adjacent door frame and wallboard. One of Evan's shoes was off his foot, lying on the floor next to his body, its laces tied. Evan was probably killed in the few minutes between his last, unanswered call to Gadlin at 1:29 am and just before 1:40 am, when Rodney called Willie to ask if he had heard something like a gunshot.

Even six years later it is almost unbearable for his parents to think about Evan's last moments alive, in what appears to have been an execution. The position of Evan's body and there being bloodstains only on the lower wall and doorframe indicate Evan was on his knees when he was shot, with the shooter standing near Evan's left side.

Phoebe Schwaegerle owned the house Evan and Carrie rented at 4082 Lyon. She arrived there at about 8:30 am with a contractor whom she wanted to look at some windows needing repair. This was supposed to be Evan's departure day from the rental. Phoebe expected him to have left the key under the mat.

She went up the steps to the front door which was slightly ajar. When no one answered her knocks, she entered, saw Evan's body, called 911 and waited for the police. The police arrived, cordoned off the scene and photographed and marked everything of evidentiary value.

They found the house almost empty. An upright vacuum cleaner stood forlornly in the middle of the living room near some trash bags waiting to be taken out. Evan's laundry was piled on the washing machine. There was a 9mm shell casing on the floor a few feet from Evan's body. Blood was pooled under him and some loose change was on the floor nearby. Evan's trousers were pulled down around his thighs. Sgt. Gantt told me people in the drug trade often hide money on their person and Gadlin may have had Evan pull down his pants to see if he had money hidden in the waistband of his shorts. Twenty two dollars in loose bills were found in one of Evan's trouser pockets—one dollar for each year of Evan's life.

Evan's wallet, car keys and cellphone were not there and never found. The bag of marijuana he took with him from Mike and Lisa's the night before was also gone. There was no sign of forced entry to the house. The front door lock and door jamb were in pristine condition. There had been no break-in; Evan had opened the door for his killer

Homicide detectives in Oakland have a heavy caseload. Each two-man team is on call 24/7 for one week and responds to new reports requiring investigation. When not on call, the detectives worked on their active cases. James "Mike" Gantt and his partner were on call and *caught* the Meisner case.

Sgt. James M. Gantt

Sergeant Gantt is an African American man in his early fifties about 5' 10" tall with a medium build. He carries himself with dignity and is soft spoken. His face is lined, with the somber expression fitting for someone enmeshed for years in the aftereffects of crime and violence.

Although not much of Mike's background came out during his trial testimony, it is extraordinary. Mike Gantt was born in Harlem and grew up in the South Bronx. He was fascinated with marine biology and hoped to become a diver, so joined the Navy. In its infinite wisdom the Navy made him an MP instead and he served four years as an MP on an aircraft carrier. A Navy friend encouraged him to join the Oakland Police Department, where he started as a patrol officer. Less than two years later he was asked to become an undercover officer and served undercover for ten years. He spent much of his undercover time making narcotics buys. He did so very successfully in neighboring cities as well as Oakland when their police force requested an undercover officer unknown to the locals. Once he was lent out for an undercover job posing as a contract *hit man* to the San Francisco Police Department, which had learned about a man looking for someone to kill his wife, whom he discovered had been cheating on him. The unhappy husband happened to know many SF officers so the SFPD had to use an outside officer. After collecting half the fee in advance Mike photographed the wife (who was in on the sting) splattered with fake blood lying in some bushes. He showed the pictures to his *client* as proof of the hit, collected the other half of the fee and the client was promptly arrested. Because their targets may search them, undercover officers usually do not carry their shields or guns when in the field. Their role is, to say the least, hazardous. Over the almost thirty years of his career Mike Gantt received many honors and medals for his work.

Sgt. Gantt arrived at the murder scene mid-morning and oversaw the technicians' collection of evidence and photography of the scene. He also oversaw fingerprint and DNA sweeps, which produced nothing material to the investigation. Sgt. Gantt returned to the office to learn what he could about Evan and begin the search for his killer.

Sometime that morning Ursula Hogan and Greg Gadlin stepped out onto their apartment balcony and saw the police cars in front of the house next door and the yellow crime scene tape blocking off Evan's rental house.

Also on that morning Rodney Fisher left his apartment next door and asked an officer if he could move his car from Evan's driveway, where it was blocked in by Evan's pickup truck. The answer was *no*. He asked the officer if *Evan is OK* and said *my friend lives there*. Rodney gave a statement to an officer about his phone call with Willie at 1:40 am. He said he went outside to check on his car after he heard what sounded like a gunshot. He also said he saw Evan vacuuming *after* having heard the shot. This obviously incorrect statement gave the jury much to talk about later.

That afternoon Sgt. Gantt called Evan's girlfriend Carrie Tully at the law office where she worked as an Executive Assistant. Gantt asked Carrie to confirm Evan was her boyfriend. When she did, he told her: *Evan has been shot, you need to come down to the precinct.* Sgt. Gantt did not say Evan had been killed, but told Carrie to come see him at the Homicide Division.

Carrie eventually found her way to Gantt's location at the Homicide Division. Panicked, she did not then make the connection between having been told Evan had been shot and the detective having directed her to *Homicide*.

Sgt. Gantt and his partner questioned Carrie in an interview room she described to me as similar to or perhaps the same as the one they used a week later to question Ursula Hogan. They asked Carrie about her relationship with Evan and where she had been the night before. The two detectives then left Carrie locked into the interview room.

After about twenty minutes they came back, showed her a photograph of Evan and asked if that was her boyfriend. She said *yes*. They looked at each other, then at her and Sgt. Gantt said: *We're sorry, your boyfriend is dead.*

Carrie managed to give the detectives Mark Meisner's name and phone number. They then left her locked in again and called Evan's father. After a while they released her and she wandered the streets of downtown Oakland in a daze.

April 1, 2011
Robin Franklin was a 23-year-old African American woman and Gadlin's first cousin. They were close enough for Robin to use Gadlin's nickname *Spoony.* I wondered where that peculiar name had come from.

Robin had serious health issues. She appeared not quite *compos mentis* on the witness stand as she struggled to understand questions and her answers were halting and disjointed. I thought she might be medicated.

Robin had been receiving $300 in disability payments on the first of every month, electronically deposited to her bank account. She used an ATM card to get access to the money. Gadlin knew about this. Gadlin called Robin several times on April 1 offering to sell her a bag of marijuana for $300. She agreed because she wanted to smoke some of the pot and sell the rest. Gadlin went to Robin's place that day with a large plastic bag, containing more than ten smaller bags of marijuana and told her she should be able to get $600 for it. In return Robin gave Gadlin her ATM card. After he left she texted Gadlin *6666*, her ATM PIN number. Gadlin used Robin's ATM card to withdraw the entire $300 from her account.

That day a local news source reported: *Evan Meisner identified as Oakland man killed on Lyon Avenue.* The report went on to say that the motive was under investigation and no suspects had been arrested.

April 2 – April 7, 2011

Robin Franklin smoked some of the marijuana she had gotten from Gadlin. On a scale of A – F she graded it an F. Carrie, Steve Bocchini and Mike Sutz had also tried the pot Evan had gotten in payment for his moonlighting job and had rated it mediocre to bad. Robin called and sent Gadlin text messages demanding he take back the pot and return her $300. Robin addressed her text messages to *Spoony.*

Gadlin agreed, picked up the pot from Robin, but did not return her money. She repeatedly texted him complaints that he now had the pot *and* her money and she had bills to pay. Gadlin never answered.

Meanwhile Sgt. Gantt pushed forward with his investigation. There was no information helpful to him in solving Evan's murder in the data bases available to the Oakland Police Department. But then Sgt. Gantt got a major break. Steve Bocchini had told Carrie about his dinner conversation with Evan hours before his murder. Carrie told Steve to call Sgt. Gantt and gave him Gantt's number. Bocchini called and identified himself to Gantt as a friend of Evan's who had had dinner with him the evening before Evan was killed. Steve told Sgt. Gantt Evan was planning to sell pot that night to a large black man, a neighbor recently released from prison and on parole.

Sgt. Gantt called Evan's father, Mark Meisner. He told Sgt. Gantt Evan's cellphone was one of four in a Family Plan Mark paid for. Since the account was in Mark's name, he could get Evan's call records. Sgt. Gantt soon had the call log from Evan's phone.

With Evan's cell phone records in hand Sgt. Gantt focused on Evan's incoming and outgoing calls in the days immediately before his murder. By now Sgt. Gantt had phone numbers for the key people in Evan's life--- his family, girlfriend, new and old landlords, friends, and employer. The number (510)395-7261 stood out in the records as not matching any of Evan's known contacts. The cellphone records listed thirteen calls between that number and Evan's in the seventy two hours before Evan's murder. Sgt. Gantt traced the number to Ursula Hogan, whose address was 4100 Lyon St., the 8-unit building next door to Evan and Carrie's rental.

The OPD database revealed Ursula Hogan was married to Gregory Gadlin, a black man about 5'11" tall, weighing 200 pounds, who was on parole from State Prison.

Sgt. Gantt wanted to talk to Ursula alone before talking to Gadlin. He had OPD officers watch her apartment for an opportunity to get to Ursula without Gadlin around. They had to wait three days. On April 7 Gadlin finally left the apartment in the morning to buy *blunt wraps* (packaged cigar tubes often filled with pot) at a nearby store.

With Gadlin away from the apartment the officers knocked on Ursula's door and asked if she would be willing to come to the OPD for an interview. (Sgt. Gantt had instructed them to say nothing about investigating Evan's murder.) She agreed and was taken to an OPD interview room set up for video and audio recording. (Ursula claimed at trial she did not think she had any choice about whether to go with the officers.) The interview room was about six by ten feet with plain walls, a cement or tile floor, one small table and several uncomfortable looking chairs. It is not clear whether Ursula knew her interview was being recorded; the detectives did not tell her.

Sgt. Gantt and his partner did not reveal anything to Ursula about her husband being a potential suspect in Evan's murder. Ursula acknowledged the (510)395-7261 number was hers—or at least used to be hers. She had gotten a new cellphone with a different number and given her old one with the 7261 number to her husband, Greg Gadlin.

The detectives asked about the night of March 30/31. She told Sgt. Gantt she was a *hard sleeper*. She took numerous medications, including tranquilizers and Ambien, which *knocked her out*. Because of the impact these medications had on her, she did not know if Gadlin had left the bed they shared that night. She said Gadlin had *encouraged her* to take her medications when they were going to bed at about 10 pm on March 30.

Sgt. Gantt asked: *Is it possible he [Gadlin] left?* She answered: *It's a strong possibility he may have left the house.* Ursula awoke from a *deep sleep* the morning of March 31

Sgt. Gantt left Ursula in the OPD interview room and called Mark Meissner. He said: *We got him.*

In the video Ursula is shown wearing a loose house dress--like a Hawaiian Muumuu—with her upper arms bare. The detectives saw severe bruising on Ursula's upper arms and asked her what had happened. Ursula said she *bruises easily* and had fallen trying to fix a windshield wiper on her car. Sgt. Gantt replied he had been *doing this* for many years and those bruises were not from a fall. (Photographs showed what looked like bruises from four fingers on one side of each upper arm and a corresponding thumb mark on the other.) Ursula eventually admitted Gadlin had bruised her arms, but claimed that happened when Gadlin had restrained her from attacking him.

Sgt. Gantt left the interrogation room and had patrol officers go to 4100 Lyon St. and arrest Gadlin for domestic violence. Gantt told the team to say nothing about Gadlin being a suspect in Evan's murder. The team arrested Gadlin uneventfully at Ursula's apartment. They found car keys, Ursula's old Kyocera cellphone with the 7261 number and miscellaneous papers in Gadlin's pockets. Among those papers was a DMV form transferring ownership of a 2005 Infiniti from Ursula Hogan to Greg Gadlin, with (510)395-7261 filled in as his phone number. The team took Gadlin to the Oakland City Jail

Sgt. Gantt decided not to talk to Gadlin then, hoping Gadlin would make a call from jail revealing something important. This was a tactic Mike Gantt had successfully used before, so he directed the jail staff put Gadlin in a cell with a phone available for inmates to use. There were large signs on the wall by these phones saying: *All inmate calls are recorded.* Sgt. Gantt told the jail personnel to let him know if Gadlin made any significant calls from jail.

This was on April 7.

At about 11:15 pm Gadlin placed a call on one of the inmate phones. The first thing a recipient hears when an inmate calls from a jail phone is a recorded voice:

> *This is a call from an inmate at Oakland City Jail. If you wish to accept the call press 1, if you do not, press 5.*

Gadlin's call was to Lou Wood, an old acquaintance. Wood is a late-40's African American man who moved slowly and spoke hesitantly in a resonant, deep voice. Lou had known Gadlin for twenty years; they had grown up together. Lou even knew Gadlin's nickname *Spoony.* He had visited Ursula and Gadlin at their Lyon Street apartment a few times to counsel them about their marital problems. Lou was a former AAA tow truck driver who knew how to get into locked cars. He had been awakened by Gadlin's call, heard the automated message inserted by the jail, pressed "1" and accepted Gadlin's call, which lasted eighteen minutes.

Gadlin told Lou he had been arrested on some *bullshit assault charge,* and could not reach Ursula. (Unbeknownst to Gadlin, Ursula had been ensconced in Sgt. Gantt's interview room most of the day.) Gadlin complained he could not remember phone numbers he needed because they were on his phone, which had been taken away when he was arrested. Gadlin did most of the talking, using some variant of *motherfucker* in virtually every sentence. Lou said little, often grunting in response. Gadlin told Lou: *You know how to get into the trunk of a locked car.* They talked about the difference between getting into the passenger area versus the trunk.

Gadlin said he needed Lou to do him a huge favor--go to the Infiniti parked in the carport at his Lyon St. apartment and get *something* out from under a white box in the trunk. Gadlin said: *Hopefully man...there be something left up in there. I think it is. Cause...they didn't find nothing.* Lou fretted about whether an onlooker seeing him breaking into Gadlin's car would call the police. Gadlin tried to reassure Lou that would not happen.

Gadlin insisted Lou to do this right away—that night. Over the background sound of a crying baby Lou said his baby was with him and he could not leave her alone. After much back and forth Gadlin reluctantly accepted Lou would not go to the Infiniti until the next morning. Lou went back to sleep and never followed through.

At trial Lou listened to the taped call along with the rest of us. He identified his voice and Gadlin's as those on the tape. One of the few light moments during trial came from the DA's final question to Lou:

Is there anything you would like to add about this call from Gadlin?

Lou answered:

Yeah, I should have hit 5...

and walked out of the courtroom.

Karen Sterling was the technician at the Oakland City Jail with the unenviable job of listening to inmates' recorded telephone calls. She listened to the recording of Gadlin's call to Lou the next morning, April 8. Recognizing its significance, she called Sgt. Gantt and played the 18-minute recording for him over the phone. Sgt. Gantt immediately instructed the Beat officer to find the purple Infiniti and *sit on it*. The beat cop found the Infiniti in the carport of 4100 Lyon within fifteen minutes and made sure no one went near it.

Knowing Gadlin had car keys in his pocket when he was arrested, Gantt checked them out of the property department and went to 4100 Lyon. (He did not need a warrant to search the Infiniti because a condition of Gadlin's parole had been his consent to searches of himself, his car and possessions.) The carport had spaces for four cars. A purple Infiniti was parked nose in, with its passenger side about a foot from the solid wall on the right side of the carport.

The car on the right is where the Infiniti was parked

Sgt. Gantt used the key taken from Gadlin's pocket to open the Infiniti's locked trunk. The trunk was crammed with old clothing, cans and miscellaneous junk, with a white box on top of the pile.

There were letters to and from Gadlin and other personal papers in the white box. Gadlin had handwritten (510)395-7261 on some of these as his phone number--the same phone number Evan Meisner had exchanged eight calls with in the hours before he was shot.

Under the white box was a Taurus 9mm automatic pistol with a live round in the chamber and fourteen rounds in the magazine. There were no fingerprints or DNA on it. It was photographed in place, bagged, marked, and put into the OPD evidence locker.

A similar Taurus 9mm

Sgt. Gantt later gave the ATF the serial number of the Taurus 9mm to find out anything he could about its history. The ATF reported the gun had been registered in Virginia to someone who moved to California and had to give it up because of a domestic violence arrest. The next owner lost it in a poker game, ending its recorded history.

Todd Weller was a criminalist with sixteen years' experience in the Oakland Police Department specializing in firearms. The DA questioned him to establish his qualifications as an expert. Weller has Bachelors and Masters degrees and a year of specialized ballistics training. He had qualified as an expert witness in many trials. When the DA ended his exploration of Weller's qualifications. Judge Nakahara asked if the PD would stipulate to Weller testifying as an expert. The PD declined and instead embarked on a series of questions designed to show forensic ballistics work is not *science*, but merely *opinion*. I watched them perform this minuet with amusement and the distinct sense these two had danced this dance before. They had. It reminded me of a not very significant but enjoyable trial moment I had getting an economist to concede economics was a combination of science and art.

The legal significance of this skirmish is that witnesses qualified as *experts* are allowed to offer opinions on matters within the scope of their expertise. For example, whether the 9mm Taurus taken from the Infiniti's trunk had fired the shell casing found near Evan's body.

Weller was good natured and made some interesting points during PD Arroyo's cross examination. One was that firearms experts were required to regularly examine and opine on unknown bullet fragments and shell casings sent to them and were then graded on the accuracy of their findings. Another had to do with *rifling*, the marks left on shell casings by the spiral grooves machined into gun barrels to make bullets aerodynamically stable and accurate. Weller testified about studies done with gun barrels taken off a production line and tested. The studies showed even consecutively manufactured gun barrels left identifiably different rifling marks on shells fired through them.

PD Arroyo finally abandoned the dance and Judge Nakahara allowed Weller to testify as an expert. However, by challenging Weller the PD had preserved the issue for appeal. (After trial he told me it would be a cold day in Hell when a Court of Appeal excluded a forensic ballistics expert's opinion testimony as nonscientific.)

All of the bullets in the Taurus 9mm were *Win* hollow points. A hollow point has a small dimple in the bullet's tip, designed to make it shatter inside what it hits rather than pass through. The Win hollow point that killed Evan shattered in his cervical spinal cord.

Weller performed twelve test fires with the cartridges found in the Taurus. He compared the markings left on those to the markings on the shell casing found on the floor near Evan's body. He showed us magnified photographs of the test casings next to photographs of the one found at the murder scene. He offered his opinion that the test cartridges had been fired from the same gun that fired the cartridge found alongside Evan's body. The markings in the pictures looked the same to me.

Weller fired some of those test rounds into a device that *caught* the bullets in something like a spider's web. Although the bullet retrieved from Evan's body had shattered, one fragment was large enough for identification. The markings on the test rounds closely matched those on that fragment. Based on these observations Weller testified the Taurus 9mm retrieved from Gadlin's Infiniti fired the bullet that killed Evan.

The DA ended his questioning by having Weller testify that the defense could have had its own expert test the gun found in the Infiniti. I wrote in my notes: *presumably they didn't*. They had not.

The PD did not score any significant points on cross, but there probably wasn't much he could have done. One small one was Weller had testified his results were subject to *peer review*. It turned out that peer review was of Weller's findings and did not involve any retest of the gun and cartridges at issue. For reasons I did not understand then or now, the PD elicited Weller's testimony the Oakland Police Department used hollow point bullets to protect anyone down range of the intended target.

Weller had shown us an interesting video animation of how when the trigger is pulled on a semiautomatic like the Taurus, it moves shells from the magazine into the barrel, fires, then ejects the casing from the side of the pistol. Judge Nakahara picked up the questioning when the attorneys were finished with Weller. I noted the carefully suppressed annoyance of both counsel. (I hated when judges asked my witnesses questions. The judge rarely knew or cared about any reason I might have had for not asking them myself—e.g., I couldn't be sure of the answers, which might hurt my client's case.) Judge Nakahara first asked Weller to show the video again. I did not see any reason for this and thought the Judge was only satisfying his personal interest. The judge then got into a technical colloquy with Weller about *ejector, extractor* and *cycling marks,* although nothing about these subjects was relevant to our case. I thought Judge Nakahara was showing off his forensic ballistics expertise for the jury.

At the beginning of the trial Judge Nakahara had invited jurors to submit their own questions of witnesses in writing. When the attorneys and judge had finished with a witness, the judge asked jurors to submit any questions they had. Many jurors did, some had questions for almost every witness. Jurors passed their written questions to Bervin, who would deliver them to the judge. Judge Nakahara reviewed them and decided which to ask and/or reword as he deemed necessary. In my civil trial practice few judges invited juror questions. Those who did allow jurors to submit questions would review them privately with counsel before deciding which to reword or allow to be asked. Judge Nakahara made these decisions without consultation with counsel. I know he reworded at least some questions because I had submitted questions of two witnesses which were not asked in the form I had written. (I remember that, but not what my questions had been.) About halfway through the trial Judge Nakahara became impatient with the many juror questions he was getting and announced he was going to drop the practice for future trials. I wondered if he was kidding.

April 11 – April 14, 2011

Todd Weller, the ballistics expert, told Sgt. Gantt the Taurus 9mm from the Infiniti's trunk was the murder weapon on April 11. Sgt. Gantt then went to the jail to interview Gadlin for the first time. He said nothing about the murder at the beginning of his interview, focusing instead on matters related to the assault charge. Sgt. Gantt showed Gadlin pictures of Ursula's bruises and pressed him about whether he was responsible for them. Gadlin said: *We were wrestling* and *She's a big girl, she likes that.* He asked Gadlin for his phone number and Gadlin responded (510)395-7261, the number Gantt knew was on Evan's phone records. Gadlin admitted no one else used his cellphone with that number.

Sgt. Gantt then asked Gadlin whether he knew a white guy next door who had been found dead. Gadlin related how Evan had allowed him to take stuff from the sidewalk put out as trash. Mike Gantt then asked Gadlin whether he had exchanged phone numbers with that white guy. Gadlin denied having done so. Sgt. Gantt then showed Gadlin Evan's phone records showing numerous calls between Evan and Gadlin. Gadlin responded: *Maybe Ursula called him.*

Sgt. Gantt told Gadlin: *You're not being honest with me. I think you were in a drug deal with [Evan] and it went south.* At this point Gadlin refused to talk further and demanded a lawyer. Sgt. Gantt handcuffed Gadlin and arrested him for Evan Meisner's murder.

Three days later the Oakland Police Department issued a press release.

OAKLAND POLICE SOLVE HOMICIDE CASE

Evan Meisner was shot and killed inside a residence in the 4000 block of Lyon Ave. on March 31st, 2011. His former neighbor Gregory Gadlin has been arrested and charged with his murder...Gadlin has prior convictions for robbery, and robbery appears to be the motive for this crime.

On cross examination the PD had Sgt. Gantt identify a photograph of a young man who resembled Evan Meisner brandishing what looked like a 9mm pistol in the front yard of a house. I wondered if the PD was laying the groundwork for a portrayal of Evan as something other than the nice young guy he had seemed to be so far. I saw a stir among Evan's family in the back of the courtroom and a whispered conversation between the family and the DA. Days later the DA called Chris Hill to the stand. Hill and Evan had been friends. Hill said he was the man in the photograph, which had been taken in his mother's front yard with him holding a toy gun. At trial Hill wore the same distinctive shirt he had worn in the picture. It turned out Chris Hill and Evan were Facebook friends and a copy of Hill's picture had been downloaded, put into the DA's file and later turned over to the PD in the pretrial Discovery process. Since Hill actually looked like Evan, the misidentification was a simple mistake and immediately noticed by Evan's family.

I ran into Chris Hill at Gadlin's sentencing and asked if it was a coincidence that he had worn the shirt from the photograph when he testified during trial. Chris laughingly said: *Hell no.*

As the DA prepared to *rest* the People's case Judge Nakahara told us the parties had entered into two stipulations. He directed us to consider these as facts binding on the jury:

- Gadlin had been convicted of a felony before March 31, 2011 and
- Gadlin had been released from State Prison and placed on parole on March 20, 2010 and remained on parole until his arrest on April 7, 2011.

The trial then moved on to the Defense case.

The Defendant's Case: There Was Reasonable Doubt Gregory Gadlin Murdered Evan Meisner

Gadlin had an alibi for when Evan was killed

Ursula Hogan is an African American woman in her late Forties. She is about 5'4" tall and 150 pounds. She was carefully dressed and coiffed as if for church, wore jewelry and carried a shiny handbag. You might not have recognized her as the same woman we had seen in the videotapes of her police interview five years earlier. Ursula tried to help Gadlin at trial. She failed.

Gadlin had moved into her apartment at 4100 Lyon when they married four months before Evan was murdered. Ursula's 14-year-old son Albert Pearson lived with them. Gadlin later testified ungallantly he badly needed a place to live that could be approved by his Parole Officer and decided Ursula's apartment was *it*. He also described their marriage as *rocky* and *shaky from the start.*

The door to the bedroom Ursula and Gadlin shared opened into the living room. The only exit door from the apartment was across the living room from their bedroom.

Ursula, Albert and Gadlin returned home about 7:00 pm the night of March 30 and did not leave the apartment that night. She and Gadlin went to bed at about 10:15 pm. She claimed she was awakened by Gadlin's phone blinking after midnight and picked it up to hear who was calling, while not speaking herself. She then called that number back, listened to make sure the person answering wasn't a woman, then hung up. She said Gadlin was in bed sleeping while this was going on. She did not see him leave and did not hear a gunshot that night.

Ursula dealt with the PD's questions calmly and fluently. But she was argumentative, evasive and blustery throughout the DA's cross-examination. She demanded a recess after one emotional outburst. Judge Nakahara impassively gave her ten minutes. The DA calmly questioned her from the lectern. He let Ursula's outbursts go by with a bemused smile then simply asked her to *listen to the question.* He repeatedly confronted Ursula with video clips of her interview with Sgt. Gantt a week after the murder, when Ursula did not know Sgt. Gantt was investigating a murder. What Ursula said to Sgt. Gantt starkly contradicted her trial testimony. For example:

- Video Clip 5. Ursula did not know if Gadlin left the apartment after she fell asleep. She is a *hard sleeper* and the medications she took made her drowsy. She had given her old Kyocera cell phone to Gadlin when she got a new one. The number on that phone was (510)395-7261.
- Video Clip 9. The night of March 30 Gadlin encouraged her to take her medications and she did. Sgt. Gantt asked: *Is it possible he [Gadlin] left?* Ursula responded: *It's a strong possibility he may have left the house.*
- Video Clip 11. Gadlin sometimes bought small quantities of pot from Rodney Fisher. It would be *very unusual* for Gadlin to have had a quarter pound of marijuana.

The DA asked Ursula to confirm each of those video clips had been made during her interview with Sgt. Gantt. After much prodding and

Judge Nakahara's occasional orders to answer she said she felt *under pressure* during the interview and barely remembered it.

After trial I asked the PD whether there had been any legal issues raised about the admissibility of Ursula's videotaped police interview. His strategy was for Ursula to simply acknowledge what she had told Sgt. Gantt without quibbling or denying what had happened. He coached her to do just that: *Listen carefully, make sure you understand the question, answer only what you were asked, and don't argue with the DA.* Had Ursula followed the PD's guidance the video would have been inadmissible hearsay. For example, if the DA had asked her: *Isn't it true you told Sgt. Gantt you don't know if Gadlin got up during the night?* Ursula could have answered: *Yes, that's what I told him, but I was taking a lot of medications that day and would give a different answer now.*

But Ursula did not follow the PD's pretrial guidance. She denied, argued and quibbled over every detail. That opened the door for the DA to impeach her by showing the jury Ursula's videotaped words blowing holes through Gadlin's alibi he had not left the apartment the night of the murder.

The PD probably pulled out whatever hair he had left when Ursula argued with the DA about whether she had said certain words in a videotaped segment just shown to the jury. She told the DA: *Show it again.* The DA happily complied, so we got to see and hear Ursula contradict her trial testimony again.

After trial I asked the PD whether he had asked Ursula when she was finished testifying how well she thought her testimony had gone. He had. She told George Arroyo she thought she had done so well: *He'll be coming home.*

Ursula is among the finalists in my mental competition for the worst witnesses I had ever seen. The jury believed what we had heard and seen her say on the videotapes and disbelieved almost everything she said live from the witness stand. She was literally unbelievable.

Albert Pearson was a 19-year-old slender African American young man who looked and sounded like the college student he now is. He testified he was playing video games in the living room the evening of March 30 2011 and went to sleep there on a sofa about midnight. He did not hear anything like a gunshot that night. Gadlin would have had to walk right by him to leave the apartment and Albert said he never saw Gadlin leave. But Albert acknowledged he had testified in Gadlin's first trial he was a *heavy sleeper.*

Although Gadlin had been married to Ursula only four months, Albert was attached to him enough to sometimes use *Gadlin* as his surname. The DA ended his cross-examination of Albert with this testimony--a subtle suggestion Albert was doing what he could to help his stepfather.

Rodney Fisher's crew stashed the gun in the Infiniti

Ursula had owned the purple Infiniti since 2005. It was inoperable and had been parked in the same carport slot at her Lyon Street apartment for several years. She had given the Infiniti to Gadlin as a wedding gift.

Ursula testified the car could not be effectively locked because its passenger side front window was held closed with wadded up paper. Thus anyone could get into the car by pulling out the paper and allowing that window to drop down. The trunk release button was inside the glove box, so access to the passenger compartment would effectively let anyone into the trunk.

Among those with access to the trunk were Ursula's 24-year-old son Damari Clay. Clay had last lived with Ursula in 2009, but often visited her Lyon St. apartment. She said she had seen her son Damari with guns. Damari had a criminal history and had been shot to death during a robbery some time in 2011. (I noted Ursula's willingness to throw her dead son under the bus to help Gadlin.)

She had known Rodney Fisher as a neighbor and marijuana source for some time. Ursula said Rodney Fisher had a friend called *Green Eyes* who also sold marijuana. Will Clark was another neighbor in 4700 Lyon. Ursula testified Clark was *bad news* and some of Clark's crew were using drugs in the Infiniti.

Ursula testified she and Rodney had had *casual sex*. Rodney had earlier denied having a *relationship* with Ursula. (The jury enjoyed a rare light moment during deliberations debating whether Ursula's testimony about casual sex conflicted with Rodney's testimony they had not had a relationship. It hardly mattered, but our conclusion was *no*.)

Gregory Gadlin's Testimony

Gadlin typically wore slacks with a long-sleeved collared shirt, occasionally topped with a sweater. I wondered whether the Court provided appropriate clothing for inmates on trial. The PD later told me his office kept an inventory of courtroom attire for defendants. If none fit, the PD would buy something appropriate from a used clothing store. That is what happened with Gadlin, whose courtroom attire had been purchased by his court-appointed lawyer.

The jury entered the courtroom as usual the morning the People rested their case, walking behind the table seating Gadlin and the PD. I saw Gadlin wearing a tie and sport jacket for the first time and instantly inferred he was going to testify. I was surprised since few criminal defendants take the stand. The PD told me only about one in ten of his clients had testified in his twenty years of practice. I later asked the DA how much notice he had Gadlin would testify. His answer: *Ten minutes*. (But DAs prepare for the possibility and Warren Ko had.)

Gadlin's version of his alibi

There was a palpable air of excitement in the courtroom as Gadlin took the stand. A person seated in the witness stand is about six feet away from the nearest juror and ten feet from where I sat. I noticed Bervin, the Sheriff's deputy, had moved from his usual spot behind the defense table to the jury's side of the courtroom. Bervin's new seat was much closer to the jury and between Gadlin and Evan's family members in the back of the room.

The PD started by leading Gadlin through a narrative about his *tough life*, which had led to a number of felony convictions and State Prison terms. Gadlin answered questions directly in a soft, deep voice, frequently making eye contact with the jury.

Gadlin related how he had been born in Colorado, his parents died when he was five or six years old and he moved to Oakland. He had five children. Two had been killed; a son in 2010 and a daughter in 2015. When he was released from prison on parole in 2010 he wanted to move to Modesto, but had nowhere to live there. He had known Ursula before his last prison term and married her on her birthday in late 2010. After that he had lived *off and on* in Ursula's Lyon Street apartment.

He claimed not to remember anything about the evening of March 30 except having gone to bed with Ursula about 10:15 pm. He testified he had not gotten up until the next morning and had not heard anything sounding like a gunshot during the night. He did recall Ursula screaming at him sometime between midnight and 2:00 am: *Who is this that keeps calling?* Gadlin claimed Ursula showed him his phone displaying the number that had called, but he did not recognize it.

He said he first met Evan Meisner on March 28, when Ursula saw a small refrigerator in a pile of stuff Evan was putting on the curb to be taken away. Gadlin said Evan told him he was leaving his rental house next door because of a mold problem. At Gadlin's request Evan showed him the interior because Gadlin hoping the owner would hire him to do the mold removal. Gadlin testified he often went to places listed for sale or rent to solicit handyman jobs as a way to earn cash. He testified he and Evan exchanged phone numbers so Gadlin could follow up on being hired for mold removal from Evan's rental. (Ten days after the killing Gadlin told Sgt. Gantt he had *not* exchanged phone numbers with Evan.)

Gadlin's responses to his lawyer's questions about his phone contacts with Evan:

PD: *Now, to your knowledge did you ever receive a call from Evan?*

Gadlin: *To my knowledge I haven't.*

PD: *To your knowledge did you ever call Evan?*

Gadlin: *No.*

Phone records from Evan and Gadlin's phones showed Gadlin had received six calls from Evan and placed six calls to Evan in the three days before the murder. Eight of those twelve were made within ninety minutes of Evan's murder.

On cross-examination Gadlin adamantly denied he had had *any* phone conversations with Evan, but conceded their *phones* had connected. This too clever by half parsing led to an amusing exchange about the eight calls *between the phones* the night of the murder.

DA: *Your testimony then would be that the victim was calling your phone—or excuse me. His phone was calling your phone then in the middle of the night?*

Gadlin: *I have no idea.*

DA: *No answer for that?*

Gadlin: *I have no idea.*

Rodney's crew did it

Rodney was a soft-spoken delivery truck driver with no criminal record except for once having passed a bad check, for which he served one night in jail and did a week of community service. Gadlin testified Rodney was a dealer with a crew of local enforcers.

Gadlin claimed Rodney's crew routinely stashed stuff in the Infiniti, going in and out of the car through the front passenger window. A week or so before March 30 someone in Rodney's crew told Gadlin there was a gun under the white box in the Infiniti and warned him to stay away from it. To enforce their warning Rodney's crew beat Gadlin badly on the street outside the Lyon Street apartment: *I was almost killed.* Gadlin testified he did not fight back because Rodney's crew had guns.

Gadlin explained his jailhouse call to Lou by saying he wanted Lou to get the gun out of the Infiniti in case his parole officer searched the car. On cross-examination he admitted his parole officer had not searched the car on earlier visits. He had an explanation ready though; his parole officer would have had no reason to search the car before Ursula transferred ownership to him. He was pressed on why he needed Lou's expertise to get into locked cars if it was so easy to drop the front passenger window to get in.

DA: *You never told Lou that was the way to get in?*

Gadlin: *I said I didn't tell him to do it because I didn't want everybody knowing about the window.*

When I heard this testimony I thought: *Not OK for Lou to know about the window but OK for him to know there was a gun in the car?*

The marijuana transactions with Robin

Gadlin denied any involvement in a marijuana transaction with Evan.

He went on to testify his cousin Robin Franklin needed $600 for a used car. She asked if he could get her pot for her $300 she could sell for $600. Gadlin then somehow got Rodney Fisher to give him pot he paid for with the $300 he got from Robin's disability payment. (One of the many problems the jury had with Gadlin's story was believing Rodney, who Gadlin said had ordered him beaten at gunpoint, would give Gadlin $600 worth of marijuana for $300.)

Some days later Robin complained about the quality of the pot Gadlin had brought her and asked him to return her money and take it back. Gadlin said he reluctantly agreed but had two problems. First, when he picked up the bag of pot from Robin she had already smoked a lot of it. Second, Rodney had Robin's $300, not Gadlin. Gadlin testified Rodney's best offer was to sell Robin's returned pot and give back whatever cash that brought in. That plan was interrupted by Gadlin's arrest on April 7.

Father to Father

This exchange was near the end of the PD's direct examination of Gadlin:

PD: *Let me cut to the chase. Do you know who killed Evan Meisner?*

Gadlin: *I have a strong idea.*

PD: *Do you think it's Rodney Fisher?*

Gadlin: *No, it's not Rodney Fisher, but Rodney Fisher knows.*

PD: *Do you think you know [who] did it?*

Gadlin: *He works for him.*

PD: *If I ask you straight up who do you think killed Evan Meisner what's your answer?*

Gadlin: *I don't want to say right now.*

After a break the PD followed up, asking Gadlin why with everything he had on the line he declined to name Evan's killer. Gadlin responded: *Out of fear for my family and my kids.*

Gadlin had earlier testified he had had five children, two of whom had been killed. The PD asked in a hushed courtroom:

Did you kill Evan Meisner?

Gadlin answered:

Absolutely not.

Gadlin leaned forward, stared intently past the jury at the Meisner family sitting towards the back and said to Evan's father:

[F]ather to father, [I]never killed Evan Meisner. Never would. I would not do it and could not do it. That's father to father.

Mark Meisner and the other family members stared back at Gadlin unflinchingly and expressionless. Mark barely restrained himself from standing and answering back.

Gadlin looked sincere and spoke convincingly. I was shaken by his direct appeal to Evan's father. I wondered later how long Gadlin had practiced those lines. His attorney told me after trial he had no idea what Gadlin would say.

On cross examination Gadlin acknowledged his many past felony convictions. He denied recognizing the murder weapon or knowing how to load and operate a semi-automatic. In perhaps a momentary lapse he said:

I've never operated a gun like [that]. I was more of a revolver man myself.

Gadlin testified he did not go to a hospital after being *almost killed* by Rodney's crew. Later the DA showed us Gadlin's booking photo taken about a week after the supposed beating. There were no visible signs of injury to Gadlin's face.

Closing Arguments, Friday, September 9

The District Attorney

Warren Ko walked us through the key facts and showed us pictures of Evan alive and dead. He said the evidence fell into four independent categories:

- The Victim. How Evan got the quarter pound of marijuana, what he intended to do with it, what he told Steve Bocchini about his arrangement to sell it to a neighbor he had known a short time, how Gadlin met the description Evan had given Steve and how Evan had gone back to the Lyon St. house with the marijuana intending to make that sale.
- The Phone Records. The multiple calls between Evan and Gadlin in the seventy two hours before the killing, including eight within two hours of Evan's murder.
- Gadlin's possession of marijuana after the murder. Gadlin's pushing his cousin Robin to buy a quarter pound of weed from him the day after the murder, coupled with Evan's quarter pound having disappeared.
- The weapon. The murder weapon was hidden in the trunk of Gadlin's Infiniti, his call to Lou from jail.

Warren argued each category of evidence *independently* pointed to Gadlin as the killer. He further argued Ursula's trial testimony was not credible and we should rely instead on what she had said on videotape to Sgt. Gantt days after the killing.

The DA went on to discuss the jury instructions we had been given. He went over how we would have to determine whether Evan's killing was First or Second Degree Murder. On that point he briefly touched on the murky concepts of *malice aforethought* and *willful, deliberate and premeditated* in our instructions. He then went over the instruction for *Felony Murder,* which established that a killing committed during a robbery is First Degree Murder as a matter of law. He urged the jury to start that aspect of our deliberations with deciding whether Evan's killing had been a Felony Murder. We ended up doing exactly that.

Warren Ko ended by calling for Gadlin's conviction as charged. Gadlin had remained impassive during the DA's closing. Of course this was the second trial in which he had heard the case against him laid out.

It was a little after 11:00. I wondered whether the PD would wait until after lunch to begin his closing argument. I would never delay in that situation because a lawyer hates a jury taking a break with the other side's words the last they had heard. Judge Nakahara glanced down at the PD, silently asking if he wanted to begin his closing argument. The PD nodded and rose.

The Public Defender

George Arroyo moved the lectern closer to the jury box. He started with a PowerPoint showing *beyond a reasonable doubt* as the highest burden of proof the law requires. I thought the PowerPoint was canned and stale and imagined Public Defender supervisors or a consultant urging staff attorneys to use it.

I had spent over thirty years as a civil lawyer, working with the lowest level of proof on the PD's slide: *preponderance of the evidence*—often described as being 51% sure, or with the scales of justice tilted slightly in one direction. The intermediate standard of *clear and convincing* evidence requires a jury to have a *firm belief* in the *high probability* of the truth of a finding.

The PD emphasized we would have to agree on the much higher standard of *beyond a reasonable doubt* to find Gadlin guilty. This required each juror have *an abiding conviction of the truth of the charge.*

The PD reminded us the defense had no obligation to prove anything. They could have chosen to put on no witnesses or evidence since the prosecution had the sole burden to prove every element of each charged crime beyond a reasonable doubt. PD Arroyo argued the defense had introduced evidence of Gadlin's alibi and that someone else had planted the murder weapon in the Infiniti's trunk

George Arroyo then listed what he described as holes in the prosecution's case creating reasonable doubt:

- No evidence Gadlin had handled the murder weapon,
- No DNA or fingerprints linking Gadlin to the weapon or Evan's house,
- Rodney Fisher's contradictory statements,
- Unexplained footprints on and near Rodney's car parked in Evan's driveway,
- An unexplained key found on a fencepost between Evan's rental and the adjacent apartment,
- A hammer found on the floor near Evan's body suggested the possibility of a struggle,
- Gadlin had no reasonable motive to kill Evan,
- That there was no science supporting the ballistics expert's opinion the Taurus 9mm found in the Infiniti was the murder weapon. The PD showed us a picture of his 8-year-old daughter standing in front of a school science project to illustrate that even second graders knew about the importance of the scientific method. I am sure George hoped it would humanize himself (easy) and his client (difficult), and

- The Oakland Police had ignored leads and suspects. (This was perhaps a reference to Ursula and Gadlin having pointed at Rodney's crew, Green Eyes, Willie Carter, or Ursula's son Damari Clay as possible guilty parties.)

The PD concluded with a plea I routinely used at the end of my closing arguments when representing a defendant.

I won't get to speak to you again and when I conclude, Mr. Ko will have another chance to address you. While you listen to Mr. Ko, please ask yourself: "What would Mr. Arroyo say in response to this?"

The prosecution in a criminal case and plaintiff in a civil case have the last word because their side bears the burden of proof. George Arroyo sat down and Warren Ko stood to make the prosecution's rebuttal argument.

His rebuttal was brief. There was no evidence supporting Gadlin's testimony he had been beaten up or physically assaulted. The defense had brought in a red herring--the picture of a Facebook friend of Evan's brandishing a toy gun--to suggest Evan wasn't such an innocent. Gadlin's jailhouse call to Lou showed he knew there was a gun in the Infiniti and someone would have to force their way into the trunk to retrieve it. Those points debunked Gadlin and Ursula's testimony that Rodney's crew routinely used the slightly open car window to get into the Infiniti.

He closed by asking the jury to find Gadlin guilty as charged of murder in the first degree and of being a felon in possession of a firearm.

Judge Nakahara told the jury we would be instructed in the law Monday morning and then begin our deliberations. He adjourned court and we left. I had much to think about over the weekend and not a soul I was allowed to talk to about it.

Part III

Jury Deliberations

THE JURY FILED into the courtroom on Monday morning September 12 to find 3-ring binders on our assigned seats. The binders held copies of the legal instructions we were to use during our deliberations and the formal charges against Gadlin. Instructions are often complicated and confusing statements of the law jurors must follow. Ours had been taken from a compendium known as CALJIC (California Jury Instructions Criminal.) I knew most had been the subject of court decisions. Many included wording taken from binding interpretations of the law such as California Supreme Court decisions. The fourteen pages of instructions we were given:

- Told the jury its role as fact finders,
- Directed us to limit our consideration to evidence presented in the courtroom,
- Explained *direct* versus *circumstantial* evidence. This one is worthy of an aside. Here is the judge's homespun explanation of the difference. Seeing your child eat a slice of chocolate cake is *direct* evidence. Coming into the room, finding a slice of cake missing, and seeing your child with chocolate on her face is *circumstantial* evidence, from which the *fact* of her having eaten the cake can be inferred.
- Provided guidance as to when a witness' credibility could be questioned. For example if we believed a witness was untruthful in some of her testimony, we could question all of her testimony and could discount testimony from a witness convicted of a felony.
- Defined the crimes of murder, felony murder and robbery.

I did not share with the other jurors I knew the California Court of Appeal, which reviewed trial court judgments, often overturned a guilty verdict if it concluded a trial judge had not given the jury the correct instructions. I also did not tell them Judge Nakahara had probably decided which instructions we would be given after considering competing sets proffered by the DA and PD. Either side might also have suggested modifications to the standard CALJIC wording of particular instructions. The judge typically allowed each side to argue why their proposed instructions should be used. This process always took place outside the presence of the jury and could easily take half a day.

After trial I found out the PD had requested our jury instructions be taken from CALCRIM, a newer alternative to CALJIC, because he thought them more understandable. Judge Nakahara refused. There are few things trial judges like less than being slapped down by an appellate court. CALJIC instructions were older and more established, meaning they had been reviewed by more appellate courts than the newer CALCRIM versions. This may explain why Judge Nakahara stuck with CALJIC, rather than venture onto what he might have thought thinner ice.

Judge Nakahara slowly read the fourteen pages of instructions to the jury as the DA and PD followed along. This took forty five minutes. Any variance from this ritual could invite appellate court scrutiny.

Some judges refused to give juries written copies of the Instructions they were to be guided by. This practice was indefensible. Some jury instructions are complex, with multiple paragraphs and subparts. Some are subtle and require careful reading and re-reading. Even with my thirty five years of litigation and trial experience I could not have accurately recalled the critical wording of many of the instructions we had been given.

For example, the most critical instruction in a criminal case establishes the presumption of innocence cloaking all defendants and defines what constitutes *reasonable doubt* about his guilt. It read:

A defendant in a criminal action is presumed to be innocent until the contrary is proved, and in case of a reasonable doubt whether his guilt is satisfactorily shown, he is entitled to a verdict of not guilty. This presumption places upon the People the burden of proving him guilty beyond a reasonable doubt.

Reasonable doubt is defined as follows:

> *It is not a mere possible doubt; because everything in human affairs is open to some possible or imaginary doubt. It is that state of the case which after the entire comparison and consideration of all the evidence, leaves the minds of the jurors in that condition that they cannot say they feel an abiding conviction of the truth of the charge.*

Try to wrap your mind around that language. By contrast the parallel instruction used in some federal courts simply instructs jurors they must be *firmly convinced the defendant is guilty.*

Judge Nakahara followed another ritual after he was finished reading the instructions. He ordered Bervin, the Deputy Sheriff who had been our guide and guard to stand and swear to watch over the jury while it deliberated. Judge Nakahara then told the three alternate jurors to stay behind for further guidance and directed the twelve of us to retire to the deliberation room and select a foreman. (He probably said *foreperson* in light of local political sensitivities.) He said nothing about what the foreman's role should be.

My pulse was racing as we stood, filed by the DA, PD and Gadlin and headed up the stairs. The weight of responsibility I felt when I realized I was going to be on the jury reached a new level of intensity.

Day One

There was more space in the jury deliberation room as we settled around the conference table without the three alternates. Bervin showed us *our* refrigerator, coffee maker and rest rooms and told us he would bring in Chinese food for lunch. Then he left, closing the door behind him. We were free to talk about the case for the first time since we had shown up three weeks earlier for jury service. I was anxious to begin and assumed the other jurors were as well.

Someone said: *We need to pick a foreman; does anyone want to do it?* Everyone looked at each other. No one spoke. Eventually I said: *I'm willing to do it if that's what you all want.* Several jurors quickly responded something like *great*, or *that's done.* No one objected. The truth is I had thought for days about how the deliberation process should be organized and would have been disappointed *not* to have been chosen as foreman. While I had no experience as a juror, I had a great deal of experience leading groups of strong-willed lawyers and mediating between contending litigation parties. Most importantly I wanted to make sure the jury engaged in a thorough discussion of the evidence before jurors staked out positions on guilt or innocence from which they might be reluctant to back down.

I asked everyone to put their first name on a folded piece of paper in front of them, since I didn't know everyone's name and assumed that was true of others. (Of course we knew the first names of the jurors we had lunch with.) Our names had only been used in the courtroom during jury selection. After that we often *became* our seat numbers—I was Juror Nine and we filed in and out of the courtroom in numerical order. After we had put out our name cards I asked if people wanted time to review their notes. We quietly did that for a few minutes.

Bervin had told us standard practice was for the foreman to communicate with the court about anything the jury might need or any questions we might have and we were to use the buzzer on the wall to contact him. Bervin left us an envelope with a list of trial exhibits and told us the court would provide any we requested. The court would also give us a laptop if we wanted to watch the video of Ursula's police interview or listen to Gadlin's jail call to Lou. We discussed which items we wanted brought up and I marked them on the exhibit list, which I signed as the form indicated: *No. 9, Foreman*. We included all exhibits any juror wanted to see, including Ursula's videos and Gadlin's jailhouse call. Some jurors asked for items we had seen or heard referred to, like drawings or police reports. I explained only the items marked on the list as exhibits had been admitted into evidence and were available for us to see.

I buzzed for Bervin and gave him the envelope. Judge Nakahara, counsel and Gadlin would have learned I was the foreman when they saw the signed exhibit list. Opposing counsel and courtroom personnel often make friendly wagers which juror would become foreman. I don't know if there was a bet this time.

It was late morning when we got to this point. I followed the approach I had thought about and recommended we not take a vote right away. I suggested instead we talk through the evidence to identify a universe of *agreed facts*. I thought the facts fell into four major categories—the Infiniti, gun, cellphone records and marijuana. I hoped our agreed facts would narrow our discussions and minimize speculation. The jury agreed and we began.

The Infiniti
I suggested we first talk about the Infiniti, since Gadlin owned it, it was the subject of his jail telephone call to Lou and the gun the ballistics expert had said was the murder weapon was found in it.

There was no whiteboard in the deliberation room, but we had an easel and a pad of 18" x 24" *butcher paper* and colored, felt tip pens. One juror appointed himself scribe and wrote notes on the butcher paper as we discussed the issues about the Infiniti. There were many photographs of the car in evidence, some taken while it was still parked in the carport, others after it had been moved to the OPD evidence yard. Many witnesses had also testified about the Infiniti. Based on all of this evidence we quickly agreed on these facts, in this order of discussion:

- The Infiniti was registered in Gadlin's name,
- The key was in his pocket when he was arrested,
- The car had been inoperable and parked in Ursula's carport slot for several years,
- The interior front passenger door handle was broken and
- The passenger side of the Infiniti was at most twelve inches from the carport's cement wall.

We then moved to logical conclusions we could draw from those facts. We did that by framing questions for discussion. The first:

- Did Gadlin believe when he called Lou from jail the only way to get into the car without a key was by breaking in?

Our answer: *YES.*

The second group of related questions had to do with whether it was *possible* for someone without a key to get into the Infiniti while it was parked in the carport:

- Was there enough room between the passenger side of the Infiniti and the carport wall to open the front passenger door?

Our answer: NO.

We discussed this more difficult question at length:

- Was there any evidence anyone had used the partially open front passenger window to get into the passenger compartment?

Ursula and Gadlin had pushed this theory from the witness stand. Our discussion zeroed in on the three main reasons we did not buy it. First, photographs taken before the Infiniti was moved from the carport showed a uniformly heavy coating of dust covering it, including the passenger side and front passenger window. Those photographs did not show any markings or disturbances in the dust one would expect to see if someone had handled the window, much less slithered in through the opened passenger side window. Second, even if someone had managed to *lower* the window to get in, he could not have *raised* it back into place from outside the car. Third, if Gadlin knew, as he claimed, that anyone could get into the Infiniti through its partially open window, why had he talked to Lou in his jailhouse call about needing Lou's *AAA* expertise to break into locked cars?

Our answer: NO.

The final question we discussed in this *accessibility* line:

- Was there any evidence *anyone* went into the Infiniti through the passenger door or its window from the time of the murder until Gadlin's arrest a week later?

Our answer: NO.

The necessary implication of that answer was only someone with the Infiniti's key could have put the gun into the trunk. Trial testimony had established Ursula and Gadlin only had one set of keys for the Infiniti and it was in Gadlin's pocket when he was arrested.

The final issue we discussed about the Infiniti got uncomfortably close to the ultimate question:

- Was there any evidence anyone other than Gadlin was involved in putting the gun in the Infiniti's trunk?

Gadlin had testified Rodney's *crew* had told him *they* had hidden a gun under the white box in the trunk. We first discussed whether anyone believed Gadlin's story. No one had.

Our answer: NO.

Our scribe then taped the butcher paper outlining the *Infiniti* issues on the wall. (After the verdict had been formally entered and we had been excused Judge Nakahara allowed me to photograph most of our butcher paper notes.)

Jury Note: The Infiniti

As we got ready to move on to another topic Bervin knocked to tell us our takeout Chinese food lunch had arrived. One juror went to buy cold drinks. We then went into the hallway where an assortment of dishes was laid out on a folding table, filled paper plates and took them back to the deliberation room. We ate at our places and after about fifteen minutes got back to work.

The gun
Having at least temporarily finished with *Infiniti* issues, I suggested we next discuss the Taurus 9mm pistol put into evidence by the DA--the gun found in the Infiniti's trunk. Todd Weller, the DA's ballistics expert had opined it fired the bullet that killed Evan.

The PD had challenged Weller about whether there was a scientific basis for his testimony the Taurus 9mm was the murder weapon. I found the *is it science* dispute unpersuasive. Whether characterized as science or expert opinion, Weller's comparisons of the shell casings and bullet fragments were convincing. Weller had relied on comparisons of test firings by that gun made with cartridges found in it to markings on the shell casing found at the murder scene and a bullet fragment recovered from Evan's body. The PD had not offered any evidence challenging whether the gun found in the Infiniti was the murder weapon. I understood the defense had no obligation to prove that or anything else. But the PD did have to get at least one juror to believe there was a *reasonable doubt* about whether the Taurus 9mm was the murder weapon. In this he failed. I was curious about whether any jurors were concerned about the subject. The heading on our next sheet of butcher paper was *The Gun*.

I started the discussion by asking: *Does anyone have any question about whether the gun in evidence killed Evan?* No one did. We then quickly agreed that:

- The murder weapon was found on April 8 in the Infiniti's trunk, and
- There were no fingerprints or DNA on the gun.

We went on to discuss another very key question, originally written on the butcher paper as:

- Gadlin knew *the* gun was in the trunk.

Our discussion quickly turned to Gadlin's testimony that Rodney's *crew* had told him they had put *a* gun in the trunk. At this early stage in our deliberations I did not want us to get to the equivalent of the ultimate question--whether Gadlin had murdered Evan--so reworded the question on the butcher paper as:

- Gadlin knew *a* gun was in the trunk.

We quickly agreed the answer to this was *yes*. However that statement did not advance the ball because it was consistent with all theories of the case: Gadlin's call to Lou from jail; his testimony about being told about a gun by Rodney's crew; and Gadlin having put the gun in the trunk sometime after killing Evan.

Jury Note: The Gun

Our scribe tore the sheet off the pad and taped it to the wall. We moved on to the next topic—the marijuana.

The marijuana

We started with the history and disposition of Evan's plastic bag of marijuana.

- Evan was paid with about a quarter pound of pot worth $600 - $800 for a moonlighting job in early March.
- Evan planned to sell the pot to raise the cash he needed to pay his $600 rent on April 1.

Mike Sutz, Carrie and Robin Franklin had all tried and *graded* the pot:

- Evan's pot was between mediocre and lousy quality.

We knew from Steve Bocchini's testimony Evan planned to sell the pot that night to an African American neighbor bigger than Evan and on parole, whom Evan had known for a short time. Gadlin fit that description. Rodney was smaller than Evan, was not on parole and Evan had known him for months. Evan and Carrie had even socialized with Rodney. Importantly, there were no cellphone calls between Rodney and Evan in the month before Evan was killed. However there were many calls between Evan and Gadlin in the seventy two hours before the murder. We rejected the defense contention Rodney was the potential pot buyer Evan described to Steve Bocchini and concluded:

- Evan was planning on selling the pot to Gadlin the evening of March 30.

The trail of Evan's bag of pot moved to Evan's new rental. His landlord, Mike Sutz saw it and sampled some:

- Mike Sutz, his new landlord helped Evan repackage a large plastic bag of pot into smaller baggies the night of March 30.

This fact led to the jury's first lengthy debate. One juror I will call *Jack* was adamant the repackaging was into one ounce baggies, which he described as *typical*. If so, the quarter pound could only have been split into four baggies, not the ten or more Robin said were in the bag she got from Gadlin. There had been no testimony *baggies* meant one ounce lots; I thought about challenging Jack's use of information from outside the courtroom, but held back. Besides, Evan's bag of marijuana had been described by different witnesses as *a quarter to half a pound, about a quarter pound*, or with hand gestures indicating something between the size of a small turkey and a quart of milk. No one had weighed it. We could not resolve the issue to Jack's satisfaction and he was adamant, so we moved on to other, less controversial points about the marijuana:

- Evan left Mike Sutz near midnight March 30 with a plastic bag holding smaller bags of pot and said he would be back in 10 – 15 minutes and
- No pot was found in 4082 Lyon St. when Evan's body was discovered

We then took up the post-murder chronology of Gadlin's dealings with his cousin Robin about a bag of pot. There was no dispute that:

- Gadlin contacted Robin on April 1 to sell her about a quarter pound of pot in exchange for Robin's $300 Disability payment,
- Gadlin delivered that pot to Robin in a plastic bag containing some number of smaller bags, and
- The pot was such poor quality Robin later insisted Gadlin take it back and return her $300.

Robin testified Gadlin called her on April 1 wanting to make that sale. Gadlin's explanation was Robin had asked his help to earn $600 she needed to buy a used car. Gadlin admitted delivering a bag of pot to Robin on April 1 he claimed he had gotten from Rodney. That Gadlin ended up with both the pot and the money was confirmed by text messages between Robin and Gadlin.

The DA had several witnesses grade the quality of the pot, no doubt hoping the jury would draw a straight line from Evan to Gadlin to Robin, then back to Gadlin. The conclusion he hoped we would draw was Gadlin killed Evan, took the pot and sold it the next day to Robin for $300. There was strong circumstantial evidence it was the same marijuana:

- Ursula said in her videotaped interview it would have been *unusual* for Gadlin to have that much pot,
- All witnesses agreed the marijuana was in a large, clear plastic bag containing smaller bags,
- All witnesses who had tried the pot graded it as mediocre to bad,
- Mike Sutz helped Evan portion it into smaller bags the evening of March 30,
- Evan had the marijuana when he left Sutz near midnight and
- Evan's marijuana was never found after the murder.

I believed it was Evan's pot Gadlin took and sold to Robin, although some jurors were not convinced of that beyond a reasonable doubt. Fortunately that conclusion was not essential to our decision as to who had killed Evan.

We taped the *Marijuana* sheet of butcher paper to the wall and moved on to the cell phone records. (Unfortunately, in the post-verdict excitement I forgot to take a picture of that page.)

The cellphone records
Several witnesses had testified about how the OPD used a proprietary tool called Cellebrite to extract data from cell phones. It is described this way on their website:

Cellebrite was the first in the industry to support physical extraction while bypassing passwords, passcodes, and pattern locks from the widest variety of mobile devices.

The police used Cellebrite technology to extract the data from Gadlin's cellphone. The result was the seventy-page printout of Gadlin's call and text message records put into evidence. Jack and our scribe-juror pored through the printout and listed all the calls between Evan and Gadlin.

While they worked on this Jack asked me if the court would give us an electronic version of the cellphone record database. He wanted to reorganize and search the data. I told Jack I would ask if he insisted, but since only the printout was in evidence it was very unlikely Judge Nakahara would give us a tool to use for what would amount to independent research. We had been instructed and repeatedly reminded we were barred from independent research. (An example would be if a juror looked up something relevant to the case on the internet. That juror would have been dismissed and a mistrial ordered.) Jack reluctantly dropped his request.

There were thirteen calls between Evan and Gadlin from March 28 through the early hours of March 31 when Evan was killed. The Cellebrite printout showed the date, time and duration of each call, whether Gadlin's phone or Evan's had initiated the call and whether it had been completed.

The first was from Evan to Gadlin on March 28—the day Evan allowed Ursula and Gadlin to take the refrigerator he had put out on the curb. There were two completed calls on the 29th, the first from Gadlin to Evan, the second from Evan to Gadlin.

Evan tried to call Gadlin the afternoon of the 30th but the call was not completed. That was the day Evan's new landlords reminded him he needed $600 in cash to pay the rent on April 1. It was also the day Evan had dinner with his friend Steve Bocchini and told him about his plan to sell the pot he got for a moonlighting job to an African American neighbor on parole he had known for a couple of weeks. That evening Mike Sutz helped Evan repackage the pot into smaller baggies and tried to talk Evan out of going to sell the pot. Evan left Mike at about midnight, saying he would be back in ten to fifteen minutes.

Gadlin called Evan on March 31 at 12:13 am. This was shortly after Evan would have arrived at Lyon St. from his new place. There were seven more calls in the next hour and a quarter—three by Gadlin, four by Evan. The last--from Evan to Gadlin at 1:29 am--was unanswered and probably made while Gadlin was walking over to Evan's house. This was the last call ever made from Evan's phone.

At 1:40 am Willie Carter called his neighbor Rodney Fisher, said he had heard something like a gunshot and wondered if Rodney had heard it too. Rodney was awake and had heard the noise.

At 1:37 am Gadlin called a number in the 916 area code and talked for eight minutes. At 3:46 am Gadlin took a call from the same number lasting nineteen minutes. We did not know who was on the other end of those calls or had that 916 area code number. But I believe I found out months after the trial. (See *Unanswered Questions* below.)

The jury concluded from the call records:

- Gadlin was the one using the Kyocera cell phone Ursula had given him with the number (510)395-7261. That phone was in Gadlin's pocket when he was arrested five days after the murder. Gadlin had also written the number on a DMV form and other documents as his phone number.
- Evan planned to sell the marijuana to Gadlin. Gadlin fit the description Evan had given his friend Steve a few hours before the

murder. (A neighbor, a big African American man on parole, whom Evan had known a short time.)

- Evan left Mike Sutz and went to Lyon St. to sell the bag of pot to Gadlin

- Evan was killed between 1:29 am when he tried to call Gadlin and shortly before 1:40 am when neighbors talked about hearing a gunshot. Indeed, he almost certainly was killed before Gadlin's 1:37 am call to the 916 area code number. Evan's uncompleted call to Gadlin at 1:29 was the last use of Evan's phone. It was not found at the murder scene and was never recovered.

We tore off the cellphone page headed *Greg-Evan* and hung it on the wall.

Jury Note: Cellphone Records

The first straw vote

It was 3:30 in the afternoon, one juror had said she needed to leave early and we had made a lot of progress going through the facts. I sensed jurors were getting anxious to see where we stood so asked if people wanted to take a straw vote. All did. I remained concerned that if people voiced their opinions they might be reluctant to change their minds after more discussion. I suggested no one *say* what their vote was but simply write *guilty*, *not guilty*, or *undecided* on a piece of paper and pass it to me. All did. Feeling both worried about a potentially serious split and excited about what the outcome would be, I unfolded the twelve *ballots* into what turned into two very uneven piles. The jury watched intently as I read out each vote. There were eleven *guilty* and one *undecided*. Jack quickly volunteered he had cast the undecided vote.

Jack is a slender, tall man in his mid-30s with some kind of tech job. He was soft spoken and friendly. He always worked on his laptop in the deliberation room before our courtroom sessions and during breaks. Every time I glanced down as I walked past in our small room Jack was staring intently at and making entries onto an Excel spreadsheet. I came to think of him as the *spreadsheet guy*.

After the straw vote jurors asked Jack to explain why he was undecided. He answered he believed Gadlin *had* murdered Evan, but was not yet *comfortable* with voting guilty. He was vague about why. After a few desultory minutes of conversation, I noted it was 4:00 pm and since a juror needed to leave early, we would quit for the day. We buzzed Bervin and told him we were adjourning. Bervin seemed surprised and perhaps a little concerned about our early day, but graciously acceded.

Day Two

I brought in a big box of donuts and we began our deliberations at 9:30 in the morning. That Jack was the focus of all attention did not seem to faze him.

Was Gadlin the killer?

Jack never said he thought Gadlin was not guilty. However Jack repeatedly said he would be *uncomfortable* voting guilty until certain *issues* had been clarified. We quickly tried to pin Jack down—what exactly were those issues? Jack's concerns were an elusive target though, as his focus bounced from one thing to another.

A real issue was whether Rodney had been involved in any way with Evan's murder. There were myriad discrepancies in Rodney's testimony, most significantly his initial statement the day Evan's murder was discovered that he had gone outside and seen Evan vacuuming *after* he had heard the shot about 1:40 am. He recanted that version a year later in a follow-up interview with Sgt. Gantt both described as intense, with Gantt shouting at Rodney. During that interview Rodney for the first time said when he went outside after hearing the shot he saw someone run across Evan's back yard toward the back fence. Rodney said while he could not recognize him, the person he had seen was an African American man, Gadlin's size, wearing a hoody.

No one on the jury wholly believed Rodney. We thought he was mistaken about *when* he had seen Evan vacuuming and probably made up the backyard sighting because he thought that's what Sgt. Gantt wanted to hear. (Sgt. Gantt told me after trial he believed Rodney told the truth about his backyard sighting and had not revealed it earlier because he was afraid he would be tagged as a *snitch*. Having a reputation as a snitch in this part of Oakland could be a death sentence.) I reminded the other jurors the DA had not mentioned Rodney's backyard sighting testimony in his closing argument. That suggested the DA didn't put any credence in it and/or had concluded we could get to a guilty verdict without him relying on a weak witness' testimony.

I told Jack we need not credit any of Rodney's testimony. The only significant evidence Rodney had contributed was his call to Willie Carter at 1:40 am about having heard a shot. The call established the time of the killing. Everything about that call was confirmed by Carter and the call record the OPD officer saw on Rodney's phone the day after the murder. Thus Rodney's credibility and the changing versions he had related were irrelevant.

I also reminded Jack there was no record of any phone calls between Evan and Rodney in the weeks before the murder and Rodney did not fit Evan's description of the man Evan said he was going to sell the marijuana to during his dinner with Steve Bocchini. Gadlin fit it perfectly. We went round and round, with my irritation toward what I saw as Jack's irrationality building. I recognized the danger of creating an irreparable rift, so leaned back and shut up while other jurors picked up the debate with Jack.

Jack struggled to accept the idea of simply discounting Rodney's unreliable testimony. As he did with other issues, Jack seemed to need every bit of evidence to fit neatly into a box, as if we were working on a spreadsheet.

Eventually Jack conceded that while he *suspected* Rodney might be involved, there was no *evidence* supporting his theory. Even Jack rejected Gadlin's testimony Rodney's crew had hidden the murder weapon in the Infiniti's trunk and severely beaten Gadlin to warn him to keep quiet about it.

The jury had spent a lot of time debating how many baggies of marijuana there were. Jack adamantly argued these were typically in one ounce lots, thus Evan's quarter pound could not have been split into the ten or more baggies Robin said she had gotten from Gadlin. Jack seemed to be basing his opinions on personal knowledge of how pot was packaged. This was another factual issue that did not fit neatly into a spreadsheet.

Another issue Jack brought up was annoyingly irrelevant. (At least to me.) The Oakland Jail technician testified she relayed Gadlin's jailhouse call to Sgt. Gantt at 8:30 the morning after the call. Gantt testified he got the call about 10 am. Jack was *concerned* about this *discrepancy* and had to be talked down by other jurors. They, far more patiently than I could, explained how people's recollections of what time something happened were often inaccurate. There was no dispute Sgt. Gantt was told about the call by the technician and reacted by ordering local patrol officers to find the Infiniti and *sit on it*. The exact time Gantt got that call was utterly immaterial. Nevertheless, it took about an hour to resolve this one *issue*. I wasn't the only one annoyed with Jack's nitpicking. Everyone else was able to comprehend the insignificance of exactly when Sgt. Gantt learned of the jailhouse call. Why couldn't Jack?

It was now about noon. Bervin buzzed to tell us he was ready to take the jury to lunch at a nearby Thai restaurant. We followed Bervin down to the basement and through the bowels of the courthouse to a van for the half mile drive to a nearby Thai restaurant. The jury sat at one large round table; Bervin sat alone, ten feet away, a mother hen watching over her brood. Amusingly, the menus we were given were headed *Juror Menu*. It didn't take a genius to figure out the court routinely brought juries there for lunch. Bervin told us Judge Nakahara requested we not talk about the case over lunch, so we chatted about inconsequential matters. I sat next to Jack and we managed to have a pleasant conversation. An hour later we were back at work in the deliberation room.

Various jurors took the lead trying to pin Jack down on and resolve his concerns. His answers flitted back and forth among issues we had already discussed and, I thought, already resolved. Jack finally said something like: *Well, if the consensus of the eleven of you is Gadlin is guilty, I can go along with that.* I responded sharply, saying we were not going to do anything by *consensus.* We each had an individual responsibility to determine if Gadlin was guilty beyond a reasonable doubt. I asked the jurors to review an instruction we had been given by Judge Nakahara, which read in part:

The People and the defendant are entitled to the individual opinion of each juror... Each of you must decide the case for yourself, but should do so only after discussing the evidence and instructions with the other jurors

I told the other jurors it was likely we would be polled after delivering our verdict. In other words, every one of us would be asked in open court whether we agreed with the verdict just delivered. Thus we would have to continue deliberating until every one of us was prepared to answer that question *yes*.

And so we did.

Jack said during deliberations he found it hard to believe someone would commit a murder for $600 worth of marijuana. (Sgt. Gantt had testified people were murdered in Oakland for a lot less than that.) Jack also said he believed Gadlin had committed this murder. I felt Jack's reluctance to come to a final decision arose from these conflicting thoughts, coupled with his need to plug all the evidence neatly into his mental spreadsheet.

After some meandering further discussion in which I did not participate a juror asked if everyone believed Gadlin had committed the murder. All nodded *yes*. I was shocked, looked across the table and said: *Jack, are you saying you believe beyond a reasonable doubt Gadlin did this?* He answered: *Yes.* When that pleasant surprise sank in I shifted the discussion to whether this had been first or second degree murder.

First or Second Degree Murder

Following the verdict form I had in front of me I said we next had to decide whether Evan's killing was first or second degree murder. The DA had told us in closing argument there were two routes to a verdict of first degree murder. The first was finding the killing was done *with malice aforethought*. That required consideration of the murky and poorly defined concepts of whether the killing had been *willful, deliberate and premeditated*.

The DA had recommended we instead approach the first versus second degree murder issue by deciding whether Evan's death had been committed during a robbery. If so, it was a felony murder and thus first degree murder as a matter of law.

I believed the DA's approach made sense. It would be much easier to first decide if Gadlin had committed a robbery than swim with Jack and other jurors through the murky waters of malice, willfulness, deliberation and premeditation. The path to felony murder passed only through robbery. I asked the jurors to put the instruction laying out the elements of robbery in front of them so we could begin with that.

Did Gadlin Kill Evan in the Course of a Robbery

Our sheet of butcher paper was headed *Robbery*. I had our scribe write down these bullet point summaries of the five elements of robbery from the jury instruction we had been given.

Jury Note: Elements of Robbery

Trial testimony had shown Evan's cell phone, car keys, wallet and bag of marijuana were missing from the scene. It was undisputed Evan had his car keys when he got to his rental house at 4082 Lyon because he had driven there and his truck was found parked in the driveway. It was also undisputed he had his cell phone with him because he had taken and made a number of calls in the roughly ninety minutes after he left Mike Sutz before he was killed. We also had Mike Sutz' testimony that Evan left about midnight with the bag of pot he planned to sell. We noted those items of *property* on the top of the butcher paper and started working through the legal elements of robbery. These are listed here, with a summary of our discussion of each.

1. A person had possession of property of some value however slight
   • Evan *had possession* of his wallet, car keys, cell phone and marijuana.
2. The property was taken from that person or from his immediate presence, either at the time of the taking or while the property was being carried away
   • I thought this language borderline gibberish. Evan's missing property was taken from him or his *immediate presence* before or shortly after he was killed.
3. The property was taken against the will of that person
   • Nothing suggested Evan had voluntarily *given* those items to anyone.
4. The taking or carrying away was accomplished either by force or fear to gain possession or to maintain possession.
   • Gadlin *took* Evan's property at gunpoint before killing him, or killed Evan first to *maintain possession* after Evan had handed it over.
5. The property was taken with the specific intent permanently to deprive that person of the property
   • None of the missing items were ever found. Gadlin sold a bag of pot to his cousin Robin for $300 the day after

killing Evan. That pot was packaged in a plastic bag like Evan's and there was about a quarter pound of it, like Evan's.

This discussion took about half an hour. We all agreed beyond a reasonable doubt Gadlin had committed a robbery of Evan.

Felony Murder

We then turned to the Felony Murder instruction we had been given. It read in part:

> *The unlawful killing of a human being, whether intentional, unintentional or accidental, which occurs during the commission...of the crime of robbery is murder of the first degree when the perpetrator had the specific intent to commit that crime.*

This called only for a discussion of whether Gadlin had the *specific intent* to commit the robbery. He had arranged to buy Evan's marijuana, exchanging over ten calls with Evan in the days before the killing, including eight calls within Evan's final ninety minutes alive. Gadlin went to Evan's house next door with a gun. There was no reasonable conclusion to draw from these facts other than Gadlin had gone there with the *specific intent* to commit a robbery. It took the jury no more than ten minutes to get to this point.

I told the jury that having concluded there was a robbery we had just decided Evan's killing was murder in the first degree. All nodded and we moved on.

There were only two more questions on the verdict form. The first was whether Gadlin had used a firearm; the second was whether Gadlin was a felon in possession of a weapon. We answered both very quickly— *yes* and *yes*.

I asked the jurors to affirm one last time each was convinced beyond a reasonable doubt our verdicts were correct; all did. I then filled out and signed the verdict form and buzzed Bervin. It was about 3:30. When Bervin came up to the deliberation room I told him we had a verdict. He seemed surprised, said we should *sit tight* and he would be back with information.

Bervin returned a couple of minutes later and told us it was too late to get the necessary players together for us to render our verdict. We would have to reconvene and do it the next morning. I later found out Judge Nakahara had promised the alternate jurors they could be there when the verdict came in. They had been on telephone standby and it was too late to get them back that afternoon.

I was very worried allowing things to percolate overnight might cause Jack or another juror to waver but there was nothing I could do about it. I slept very little that night, worrying about having to restart deliberations in the morning.

The Jury Renders Its Verdict

We reconvened at 9:30 am on Wednesday, September 14. The manila envelope with the verdict forms sat on the table where I had left it the day before. I checked the forms one more time and mulled over whether to ask the jury to confirm their votes. I decided not to, but our juror-scribe reminded them of what I had said about jurors being individually polled and asked if everyone still agreed with their votes of the day before. All nodded "yes". I was not the only one watching carefully for Jack's nod. There was a high level of tension in the deliberation room.

We buzzed to let Bervin know we were ready and he came to get us in a few minutes. We filed down the stairs into the courtroom in the prescribed numerical order. I carried the sealed envelope with the verdict forms. Evan's family members were sitting in their usual places in the courtroom. Gadlin's wife Ursula was not there, nor was his stepson. The three alternates were in their usual seats.

The import of what we were doing made me more nervous than I ever remember being in a courtroom. After we were seated Judge Nakahara said: *I understand there is a verdict, will the foreman raise his or her hand.* I raised my hand. The Judge said: *The record should indicate Juror Nine is the foreman.* He then asked me to give the envelope with the verdict form to Bervin, who walked over, took it from me, then handed it to Judge Nakahara. The courtroom was silent. While the Judge opened the envelope and slowly reviewed the verdict form I worried about whether I had filled it out correctly. Would Judge Nakahara tell us to go back upstairs and fix it? Instead he silently handed the verdict form to the clerk, who stood and read aloud:

Count One: *We the jury find Gregory Gadlin guilty of murder in the first degree.*
             We the jury find Gregory Gadlin used a firearm in the course of this crime.

Count Two: *We the jury find Gregory Gadlin, a convicted felon, was in possession of a firearm.*

Judge Nakahara asked counsel if they wanted the jury polled. As I had anticipated PD Arroyo said he did. The clerk asked each juror by seat number if they agreed with the verdict just rendered. Jack was juror four, seated behind and above me. I resisted a strong impulse to turn around and look at Jack when it was his turn to answer. I started breathing again when he said "yes" as did all of the jurors.

Gadlin was seated at counsel table and showed no emotion. Nor did DA Warren Ko or PD George Arroyo. The PD told me Gadlin thanked him later for doing what he could.

Judge Nakahara thanked the jury, ordered the clerk to maintain our names under seal and released us from service. He announced sentencing would take place on October 13 after a probation report had been prepared.

The judge told us we were now free to talk about the case with anyone we chose and that he, the DA and PD would be coming up to the jury deliberation room to talk with us. We filed back upstairs, this time joined by the alternates.

Part IV

After the Verdict and Sentencing

THE DELIBERATION ROOM was crowded with fifteen jurors and alternates. The adrenaline level was high, with much chattering among us. No one sat. As the three alternates looked at our butcher paper notes taped to the walls a juror asked how they would have voted. Alternates one and two quickly said *guilty*. Alternate three, the *coloring book* young woman, said *not guilty—not enough evidence*. No one bothered arguing with her

The Jury Gets to Talk to the Players

Judge Nakahara came in wearing his judicial robes, glanced at our *wallpaper* and was quickly peppered with questions as he stood by the doorway.

I asked: *What happened in Gadlin's first trial?* It had to have been a *guilty* verdict or there could have been no retrial. (Had it been *not guilty* Gadlin would have been protected from retrial by the Double Jeopardy clause of the Constitution.) Judge Nakahara dismissively characterized the Court of Appeals reversal of the verdict in Gadlin's first trial as highly technical and unwarranted. My impression was he was either unfamiliar with it or was sticking up for a colleague. No trial court judge likes being reversed.

I read the appellate court opinion overturning Gadlin's first conviction later that day. Before that trial a different judge had refused Gadlin's request to represent himself. This was the colloquy between that judge and Gadlin in 2013, two months before his first trial:

Court: *You have never represented yourself in any of the cases that you've had in the past?*
Gadlin: *No.*
Court: *Now, those cases were not as serious as this case. What is it about this case that has changed so that you would want to represent yourself on this case?*

Gadlin: *I'm just exercising my right.*
Court: *Now, presently you are represented by a very experienced at-*
            torney.... You understand that if you make this decision to
            represent yourself, you'll be giving up all of the advantages
            you might otherwise have had in having somebody with that
            experience representing you?
Gadlin: Yes.

Nevertheless, the Judge denied Gadlin's request and the trial went forward with Gadlin represented by a different public defender. I found out later the first jury had deliberated only forty five minutes and wondered how they could have discussed anything at all in that short time.

The judge's denial of Gadlin's request to represent himself was a clear violation of his Constitutional rights under a controlling 1975 US Supreme Court decision. In that decison the Supreme Court answered the question of whether denying a competent defendant the right to represent himself was an infringement of his constitutional rights with a resounding *yes*.

Forcing a lawyer upon an unwilling defendant is contrary to his basic
right to defend himself if he truly wants to do so.

Thus the appellate court had properly reversed Gadlin's first conviction for Evan Meisner's murder.

When I read the decision I wondered if Gadlin's request to represent himself had been an attempt to game the system. Had Gadlin hoped his request would be denied so he could raise the issue on appeal if he were convicted? I almost certainly was wrong about that. I learned after trial Gadlin's original PD was well known for not getting along with his clients. Gadlin probably had not liked or trusted that lawyer and so had asked to represent himself.

Someone asked Judge Nakahara what kind of sentence Gadlin would get. The judge vaguely said he would have to see the probation report before imposing sentence. I was dubious about his answer and asked how much leeway Judge Nakahara actually had, since conviction of murder in the first degree carried a prescribed sentence, as did being a felon in possession of a gun and Gadlin's status as a three strikes felon. He acknowledged these points were correct and said Gadlin had been sentenced to *triple digits* after his first trial and likely would be again. (His first sentence had been 116 years to life.)

Several prosecution witnesses had testified about how Gadlin's cell phone records had been extracted from his phone and how to interpret Cellebrite's printout. Several of our technically oriented jurors had submitted written question for those witnesses. One asked Judge Nakahara why his questions had not been posed to the witness. The judge answered he thought those questions were designed to show off how much the juror knew rather than shed light on issues material to the case. I was quite amused by his answer because I had come to the same conclusion about Judge Nakahara's questions of the prosecution's ballistics expert.

During trial we had to leave our notebooks in the courtroom at the end of each day. I asked Judge Nakahara if jurors could keep their notebooks. I was pleasantly surprised when he said *yes*. I then asked if I could photograph the butcher paper notes we had taped to the walls during deliberations. Judge Nakahara glanced around at them and said *yes*, except for ones with individuals' phone numbers. I quickly used my phone to do so. Having both my notes and photographs of the jury's notes made this book possible.

Judge Nakahara left and Warren Ko, the DA and George Arroyo, the PD came in. Warren sat down and looked relaxed, as one would expect of the winning lawyer. George stood and looked pressed for time. A juror asked the DA why he had left a lawyer (me) on the panel. He answered: *Oh, he was a civil lawyer at PG&E so it wasn't a big deal.* I tried not to feel insulted.

The DA asked if the jury had followed his suggestion that evidence fell into four independent categories:

- Evan's connection with Gadlin,
- The phone records,
- Gadlin's possession of marijuana and
- The weapon.

I pointed to our butcher paper charts on the walls and described how we had put the evidence in similar, but not exactly the same categories:

- The Infiniti,
- The gun,
- The marijuana and
- The phone records

I also explained how we had followed his suggestion we approach the issue of whether the murder was first or second degree by determining there was a robbery and getting from there to felony murder and first degree.

After trial I thought about the career challenge Warren Ko faced in this retrial as a relatively new lawyer. The first trial had been handled by a different DA, who got a conviction with the jury out only forty-five minutes. From a career perspective, Warren could at best match that result; at worst, he could end up with a hung jury or even a not guilty verdict. Warren ruefully acknowledged that assessment. In contrast, George Arroyo could not do any worse for Gadlin than his first lawyer had, so from a career perspective, this case only had upside potential.

George Arroyo told me Warren started getting antsy when our deliberations extended into a second day. Evan's family spent that time hoping no one would believe Gadlin's story and worrying why it was taking us so long

The PD asked why we had not credited Gadlin's alibi he had been in bed with Ursula or his testimony he had been beaten by Rodney's crew, who planted the gun in the Infiniti. Many jurors joined in responding we did not believe Gadlin's testimony, or Ursula's that he was in bed with her all night. On the *beat down* issue, I told George we had looked at Gadlin's booking photo, which showed no evidence of a beating. I also told the PD I had noticed he had not asked Ursula or her son Albert Pearson any questions to confirm Gadlin's beat down testimony. George, standing with his arms crossed, smiled and answered something like: *You noticed that...No I didn't.* The inference I had drawn from the defense not seeking to corroborate Gadlin was George didn't believe the story and had declined to invite his witnesses to commit perjury. The alternative explanation was George did not ask because he was afraid of the answers he might have elicited.

After the PD left Warren Ko told us Evan's family were gathered in the DA's conference room on another floor and would like to meet and thank any jurors who were so inclined. Most of the jury panel followed Warren to meet with the Meisner family, Evan's girlfriend Carrie Tully, and Steve Bocchini, the friend he had dinner with hours before he was killed.

Father to Father, Revisited

Evan's family and friends were in a conference room and welcomed the jury warmly, thanking us for our service. I told his mother Valerie how I could barely comprehend what they had gone through—learning their son had been murdered, going through the first trial, Gadlin's conviction and sentencing, his appeal, the verdict being reversed, a second trial, then waiting for another verdict. I told Steve Bocchini how important his testimony had been. Evan's father Mark Meisner was in the back of the room and eventually I worked my way over to him. Warren Ko, the DA was sitting nearby. I shook Mark's hand.

It was Wednesday, September 14. My iPhone calendar for that day had a reminder saying *RIP* because September 14 is the anniversary of my oldest daughter's death from a drug overdose. I started telling Mark Meisner how jurors had been chatting about their memorable moments from the trial. I told Mark I would never forget mine--Gadlin looking at Mark and saying *father to father I didn't kill your son*. At that moment I broke down in tears, overcome with my own father to father moment. Mark and I hugged for a long moment, then I got myself under control and moved on.

Sentencing

Sentencing was a month later on October 13. I arrived early and sat waiting on a bench in the hallway outside Department 8 on the fifth floor. Judge Nakahara walked by on his way to the courtroom, saw me and came over to chat. I complimented him on his conduct of the trial, which was more efficient than most of the civil trials I had been in. I told him about my regret at not having contact information for the other jurors. He said juries typically passed around a sheet of paper with contact information for jurors to exchange. I said I wished he had told us, because none of us had thought of it. I asked if it would be possible for me to give my contact information to the court, which could send it out to other jurors for them to decide whether to respond to me. He agreed and I later gave him a note with my information. I never got a response and doubt Judge Nakahara ever sent it out.

I walked into the courtroom and sat in the back. Evan's family were seated across the aisle in their usual places. Gadlin's wife and stepson were not there. The only other spectator was Jimmy, Alternate two. This time Gadlin was wearing green and white striped, prison-issued clothing, with orange socks. There was a large "P" stenciled on the back of his shirt. His PD, George Arroyo sat next to him. Warren Ko, the DA was in his usual seat.

Judge Nakahara took the bench and said he has read the probation report, letters from Evan's parents and friends and a letter the PD had submitted in Gadlin's behalf.

Probation Report

The probation report contained a two-page outline of Gadlin's criminal history, which began shortly before he turned thirteen. He was first committed to a juvenile correctional facility at seventeen, was first convicted as an adult at nineteen and began his first prison sentence at twenty. He served additional prison terms at ages 22, 25, 28 and 33. He was sentenced to fifteen years for the last of those crimes--robbery by a felon with a firearm. Gadlin was paroled from that sentence in 2010, the year before he killed Evan Meisner. He was on parole on March 31, 2011.

Gadlin refused to talk to the Probation Officer preparing the report. Among the aggravating factors the Probation Officer listed were that Gadlin:

- Had served five prior prison terms,
- Was on parole when the crime was committed and
- Had not been compliant with prior probation and parole terms.

After briefly summarizing the facts of Evan's murder the Report concluded:

> *Given the heinous nature of the crime, [Gadlin] should be imprisoned for the maximum term permitted.*

The PD had sent a letter to the Probation Officer, saying in part:

Mr. Gadlin, having sat through a trial for the same incident in 2013, was not surprised by the verdict but remains deeply disappointed by the outcome.

Mr. Gadlin has maintained his innocence on this matter from day one. At this trial, Mr. Gadlin testified in his own behalf with the hope members of the jury could see that he was not responsible for the murder of Evan Meisner. Mr. Gadlin did his best to explain all of the circumstantial evidence presented against him. Nevertheless, the jury convicted Mr. Gadlin as charged after several hours; spanning over a two-day period, of considerate and detailed deliberation. Mr. Gadlin is not willing to discuss this case any further at this time and would prefer to waive any interview in preparation for your report.

In the time that I have represented Mr. Gadlin over the past year, I found him to be a man who deeply cares about his family and has made serious changes in his manner of thinking, his general outlook of life, and the kind of person he wants to become. As a result, Mr. Gadlin is a different person than the man who was sentenced for these same crimes in 2013.

Valerie Meisner's Victim Impact Statement

Judge Nakahara noted he had read the family's Victim Impact Statements attached to the Probation Report. He then invited family members to address the court before sentencing Gadlin. Evan's mother stood.

The physical setup for family members to speak at sentencing was at best awkward. Valerie Meisner stood between the *bar* separating the public area of the courtroom in the rear from the front of the room, with Judge Nakahara's raised bench, counsel tables, the witness box and the jury box. Thus Valerie faced the Judge. But because she stood behind Gadlin, she was looking at his back. She approached this spot with a determined expression. With barely restrained anger she read her statement while staring intensely at the back of Gadlin's head.

Impact Statement of the Murder of My Son, Evan Meisner,
by Valerie Meisner, Mother, October 13, 2016

Defendant: Gregory Gadlin
Victim: Evan Charles Meisner
Docket # 167072
Date of Crime: 3/31/2011
Location: Oakland, CA

Forever in our Hearts

Evan Meisner
July 5, 1988 · March 31, 2011

Here we are again, Trial #2, with the same verdict of GUILTY, and with Gregory Gadlin continuing to claim his innocence. He has shown that he *cannot* even tell the truth. His sworn testimony was nothing but one lie after another. Does he really think we believe that he is the "good person" that he claims to be? Does a "good person" violate his parole by owning a handgun? Does a "good person" cause harm to his wife of less than a year? Does a "good person" steal and swindle from his cousin, a woman on disability? Does a "good person" claim to have converted from Muslim to Christianity and then spin a tale so wild that no jury member could even consider it to have an ounce of truth? Does a "good person" really expect us to believe that he--a parolee with a lifetime of felony crimes to his credit, including a home invasion and prior armed robberies, a repeat criminal—was *so* fearful of his neighbor's friends, that they beat him up "within *an inch* of his life", and then paid him $300-$400 to hide their gun in his car? One look at the booking photo only one week later tells the truth—no such event occurred. He's a liar. HE'S the one with the gun. HE'S the **bully**. He is anything **BUT** a "good person"!

Gregory Gadlin is a thief, not only of goods, but of the most valuable and precious gift created by God--people. He stole our only son from us. He stole the sound of Evan's genuine laughter from us. He stole the creativity of Evan jamming on his guitar and piano from us. He stole a brother from his sisters. He stole the chance for his now, four nieces to be loved by him. He stole the only nephew from some of his aunts. He stole a cousin and a grandson. He stole Evan's spontaneity from us. Gadlin stole **Evan's future**. He stole acts of kindness from friends that Evan would have bestowed. He stole the feeling of being-accepted-for-who-you-are from people Evan would meet. He stole contributions Evan would have made to his craft. Gadlin stole an *actual* good person, Evan Charles Meisner, from this world.

Gadlin never turned to look at her.

Mark Meisner's Victim Impact Statement

When Valerie was finished Judge Nakahara invited Evan's father to speak. Mark Meisner stood in the same spot with quiet dignity and spoke in a calm voice directed at Judge Nakahara. This is his statement.

Impact Statement as an outcome of the murder of my son, Evan Charles Meisner by Gregory Gadlin

A big bear hug and the words "Love you Pops" were the last words my son Evan spoke to me as he turned and left for his home in Oakland. "Love you too Bud" were my last words to him. Little did we know this would be the last time we would see each other in this life. A few months before, our family spent a week in Santa Cruz in celebration of my parents' 50th wedding anniversary and was able to spend some quality time being together. To many of Evan's extended family this would be the last time they would see him either. As I reflect on the last moments we shared and a lifetime of experiences, a huge void has formed in my being. We were very close in many ways and so our loss is compounded. In his youth, we loved road trips to catch fish, to compete in skating and BMX races and to vacation with the family. These were special times that allowed us to talk about life's mysteries; for a son to ask those probing questions that only a father could answer. As the warm months begin, the excitement I used to feel while preparing and experiencing those times are no more; how I miss them.

Evan was a good young man becoming something special. Hard working in the construction trade, I believe he was on course to being a business owner. Being independent, a willing taker of calculated risk, he was preparing for the opportunity. As I was going through his belongings, I found an application for a business license for "Evan Meisner Construction." He loved people and enjoyed everything life had to offer. His nature was to be spontaneous and his love of aggressive, risky sports was sincere.

When homicide sergeant Mike Gant called during the afternoon of March 31, 2011, I was horrified to learn that Evan had been murdered. The shock, anger, of this sudden reality was almost too much to bear. I was faced with having to inform his mother, sisters, and other family members of the tragedy. Every phone call I made, reliving the shock and horror over and over those hours and the days and weeks that followed were agonizing. As the hours turned to days then weeks, my sleepless and restless nights were consumed with the raw grief I was suffering.

As I learned more about Evan's last moments it was very difficult for me to relive those moments in my mind; The hope and thoughts of making rent money and moving into his new home were cut short by the horror of being confronted at gun point, forced into submission and then in a flash his spirit was released before the bullet stopped. Unfathomable; how a person can take another's life in any manner to avoid the inconvenience of a possible victim/ witness to his armed robbery of a bag of B grade marijuana, or was it more about the dominance and subjecting terror? How can a person be so callous? Well he was and there is a price to be paid once again and hopefully forever.

$22 and change, yes the amount of money found with Evan represented $1 for each year of his life. Only 22 years seems to me a little short of a life time. Surely a father should never have to outlive his children. I can think of no greater offense than to experience this. It is one thing to have a child die from an illness, or accident; even still so horrible - it is yet another when a life is taken by another person with a choice.

The family name "Meisner" will be no more when I pass. Evan would have been the only man to potentially pass our name along. Evan was the 6th generation of the "Meisner" family name from 1857 when my great-great grandfather and his family came from Germany by ship to the United States.

I find it odd that Evan loved making his home in Oakland. I think it was conveniently located to most of his social activities, work, and his closest friends. Frankly speaking, certain parts of Oakland are a war zone. The number of lives lost due to homicide rival lives taken in major cities found in Iraq and Afghanistan. With over 100 murders committed every year almost all of which go unsolved is an American tragedy. How many sons and daughters must we lose to violence? Our family has come to Oakland to work with the OPD Homicide Division, District Attorney's office, and the many visits for court dates in this trial. I have to say we have met some really terrific people trying to do their job and dealing with an awful reality. Their dedication, respect, and sensitivity to our loss and doing their professional best to right the wrong is outstanding. I think there is hope for Oakland but the city needs to commit to solving its problems and assess its priorities to fix them. I was astounded to read that the OPD Internal Affairs had 30 officers assigned, but that Homicide had 10. Perhaps these numbers should be reversed. The total number of officers is about 100 below the planned norm as well.

It is my opinion the State of California is releasing too many inmates on parole. This is evidenced by a 67% recidivism rate. For every three convicts released to parole, two of them will commit and be convicted of another crime and create another victim/s. To get to 3 strikes is yet another crime, victim and conviction. Inmates like Greg Gadlin are set free early for good time and work time. What is this? 2 strikes and you walk early? If he had been in prison for the full sentence of his last conviction, Greg Gadlin would still be serving time and we wouldn't be here. Keeping hardened career criminals separate from society is essential and tax money well spent. One of governments' primary obligations is to keep the peace. Some individuals just can't play nice and by the rules; when they can't, they should be sent to prison for a very long time with no parole.

The victims of this crime include others than Evan, his family, and friends. I worry about Greg Gadlin's family members and how they will do in the future. I sincerely hope that Greg Gadlin's example will provide motivation to determine good values and develop better character traits that contribute to society in positive ways. Greg Gadlin himself is a victim of his own doing. He will continue to have choices as he takes up residence in state prison. Perhaps he will change for the better and make a difference there. I hope that we and all past victims can put this night mare behind us and that we can all move on, yet respecting those we have lost and that which has been taken or violated in our lives by him. Please let there be no future victims by Greg Gadlin's hands.

Greg Gadlin has chosen his own destiny by demonstrating a gross disregard for the life, liberty, property, and happiness of others. He cannot restore Evan's life, nor can he eliminate the loss, pain, suffering, and grief Evan's family and friends have endured, but he can be removed from society without the possibility of returning to it. A life in prison without the possibility of parole is the only way to prevent future horror, pain, and suffering others are likely to experience if Greg Gadlin is ever released into society.

The preceding statement was made at the last sentencing hearing in 2013. My words then are the same now. This trial has brought back thoughts and emotions I have not felt for some time. Revisiting these memories has reminded me that grief is a condition that never truly goes away. We deal with it the best we can, but it is not enough; especially in cases such as Evan losing his life the way he did.

I have thought about the concept of justice, and find the legal system has the responsibility to serve justice on this earth and this life for those that choose to violate the laws of man and God. I am glad that we have such a system in this country with people that are willing to serve in that capacity. I am glad that citizens don't have to take actions to serve justice on their own as they do elsewhere.

Mark Meisner's final words were:

Please let there be no future victims at Gregory Gadlin's hands.

Mark sat down with his family. Judge Nakahara asked the PD if Gadlin wished to say anything. George Arroyo leaned over and whispered in Gadlin's ear, who shook his head *no*. Judge Nakahara said nothing about the crime or the convicted killer sitting before him and moved on with an almost mechanical discussion of sentencing.

By contrast, the Judge who presided over Gadlin's first trial said at sentencing the murder was *absolutely senseless* because the evidence showed Evan was prepared to hand over the marijuana. He went on to say the shooting *seems like it was an execution and cold-blooded and heartless* and Gadlin *should never hit the streets again*.

Sentencing
Sentencing is a complex process under California's criminal laws. For example, First Degree Murder carries a sentence of 25 years to life.

However, Gadlin fell under California's *Three Strikes* law, which tripled that to 75 years to life. His use of a firearm added 25 years and his prior sentences added an additional 17 years. Gadlin's final sentence was 117 years to life in State Prison, with a credit of 2,012 days for time served.

Judge Nakahara advised Gadlin he had sixty days within which to file a notice of appeal and the Appellate Court would appoint counsel for him if he was unable to pay. Judge Nakahara then said:

> *The judgment and sentence of the court is entered and Gregory Gadlin is remanded to the Sheriff to be remanded to the Department of Corrections.*

The Deputy led Gadlin out of the courtroom.

After sentencing I talked to the DA about why this had not been a capital case. In California the death penalty can only be imposed where there are *special circumstances* such as torture, multiple murders or lying in wait. While murder during a robbery could qualify, the District Attorney's office rarely sought the death penalty in such cases for practical reasons.

Capital cases require a jury willing to impose the death penalty. The original jury panel for the Gadlin trial was 180 people. If it had been a capital case the panel would have had to be at least twice as large to end up with a death penalty qualified jury. Another practical impediment is capital cases usually require two trials. The first determines guilt. If the defendant is found guilty with the requisite special circumstances, a second trial is conducted before the same jury to determine whether the death penalty should be imposed. The final practical reason is the last time the State of California conducted an execution was over ten years ago.

Unanswered Questions

Why did Gadlin kill Evan instead of taking the pot and leaving.

I believe Gadlin thought he had nothing to lose and possibly much to gain by killing Evan. Gadlin had already spent much of his adult life in prison and was a three strikes loser. Gadlin knew if he left Evan alive and Evan reported the crime Gadlin was going to prison for life. Conversely, if Gadlin killed Evan he might not have been caught. If he were caught Gadlin was going to prison for life. Thus, killing Evan was a rational decision-- assuming Gadlin had no compunction about taking an innocent person's life. There was a hint of a possibly darker motive though. Ursula told Sgt. Gantt Gadlin did not like white people. Thus Evan's race may have sealed his fate.

Who was on the other end of Gadlin's two post-murder calls.

I believe I know the answer—even if not *beyond a reasonable doubt*. Gadlin's phone records showed him having two conversations shortly after Evan's murder with a number in the 916 area code, which covers Sacramento. The cellphone records show Gadlin killed Evan between 1:29 am, when Evan made his last outgoing call and shortly before 1:40 am, when neighbors called each other about hearing a gunshot. Gadlin's first call with the 916 number was at 1:37 am and lasted eight minutes. The second was at 3:46 am with the same number and lasted 19 minutes. So who was on the other end of those calls?

After trial a Google search for *Gregory Gadlin* turned up 2013 reports of a Gregory *Aaron* Gadlin sentenced in Sacramento to 1,000 years in prison for a robbery spree. This was two years *after* Evan's killing.

From May 2013 through July 2013, [Gregory Aaron] Gadlin was engaged in a robbery crime spree involving primarily convenience stores and gas stations. Gadlin would typically display a handgun and rob employees of money and personal belongings. During one robbery Gadlin fired at the clerk and missed. Three days later in another robbery, Gadlin shot a store clerk in the torso and hand.

Gregory Aaron Gadlin had three prior felony strike offenses on his record and was on parole at the time of these crimes. His criminal history obviously had begun well before 2013.

The final piece of the puzzle fell into place when Stephanie Bonner, Gregory D. Gadlin's ex-wife, told me Gregory Aaron Gadlin is Gadlin's son *Junior.* Stephanie had cared for Junior as an infant and knew he lived in the Sacramento area. Assuming the post-murder calls were between Gadlin and Junior, what were these father and son career criminals talking about in the middle of the night minutes after Gadlin had killed someone? Whatever it may have been, it's fair to say *the apple did not fall far from the tree.*

Part V

Final Thoughts

S ADLY, FOR EVAN's family and loved ones, Gadlin's sentence of 117 years to life may be illusory. Over ten years ago Federal judges had found overcrowding in California's prisons constituted *cruel and unusual punishment* under the Eighth Amendment. The result was a panel of federal judges now control major elements of state prison administration. In 2014 that panel ordered California to implement an *Elderly Parole Program*. That program makes inmates who are over sixty years old and have served at least twenty-five years of their sentence eligible for parole. The Meisner family was recently formally notified Gadlin would be eligible for parole in 2036, twenty-five years after Gadlin was incarcerated for Evan's killing. Gadlin would then be seventy-three years-old. If alive and able Mark Meisner vows to be there to oppose another parole.

Mark and Valerie Meisner maintain a close friendship with Carrie and her baby. They take pride in friends and family members who have used the name *Evan* for new babies. Mark is an active participant in a grief support group. Valerie tries to stay focused on the future and her teaching.

I went into jury service with a cynical view of the criminal justice system as a pre-trial plea bargain mill and venue for rote proceedings for cases going to trial. This experience did not shed any light on plea bargaining, but I was entirely wrong about the trial side. First, my fellow jurors were unfailingly serious about embracing their roles as citizens exercising life-changing power over the defendant as well as the victim's family and loved ones. Second, the players in the drama-- judge, lawyers, sheriff's deputy, court personnel and testifying law enforcement personnel--were all competent, dedicated professionals.

The court could do a better job of explaining certain things to jurors. Here are two examples. One, explain to juries how the peremptory challenge process works. Two, give juries some guidance about what the foreman's role should be during deliberations.

It is a tribute to Judge Nakahara and the lawyers involved that the trial was conducted so efficiently—more so than most of the civil trials in which I participated. Civil litigation has orders of magnitude more pretrial motion practice, "discovery" and paperwork in general than this case had. (I could find only one written pre-trial motion regarding an evidentiary issue—the one involving Steve Bocchini's hearsay testimony.) Although tempted I will forebear from concluding there is an inverse relationship between pre-trial paperwork and trial efficiency.

I had left lawyers on jury panels several times when I thought they would be fair, although I knew they would likely end up as foremen. (They did.) I did not end up regretting those choices. Based on my experience in this trial, if I were still in practice I would add another criterion to that analysis: Am I comfortable this lawyer/juror will be sitting there during trial trying to figure out why I'm trying the case the way I am and possibly writing about it later?

If the facts of this case as I describe them seem to point to an inevitable conclusion Gadlin was guilty, that result was not clear to this juror until we on the jury had talked through the facts and law together during our deliberations.

Greg Gadlin will hopefully spend the rest of his life in an environment he is thoroughly familiar with--state prison. Evan Meisner's family and loved ones will spend the rest of their lives missing him and mourning his loss.

Acknowledgments

I THANK AND acknowledge Alameda County Deputy District Attorney Warren Ko, Alameda County Assistant Public Defender George Arroyo, Oakland Police Department Sergeant James (Mike) Gantt, Mark and Valerie Meisner, Carrie Tully and Steve Bocchini for meeting with me after trial to flesh out what had happened in and out of the courtroom, before and after trial and for helping me understand more about Evan Meisner. I also thank and acknowledge Stephanie Bonner, Gadlin's ex-wife and mother of three of his children for talking with me. I also read Stephanie's book about her life: *Uncovered Me, Losing to Win*.

A special thanks to Bill Cole, a friend, criminal defense attorney practicing in Alameda County and frequent breakfast companion, who badgered me into writing this book.

About the Author

D AVID H. FLEISIG is passionate about the law. A retired civil trial lawyer, he earned a BS in chemistry, an MBA, and a law degree from the University of California, Berkeley.

With more than thirty-five years of legal experience, he occasionally serves as a volunteer Judge Pro Tem, hearing small claims cases and mediating settlements. In *People v. Gadlin,* he served as Juror Nine and the jury foreman.

CPSIA information can be obtained
at www.ICGtesting.com
Printed in the USA
JSHW021411060420
5008JS00004B/1074